Embracing
Change

Embracing Change

ESSENTIAL STEPS TO MAKE YOUR FUTURE TODAY

TONY BUZAN

ACTIVE

Educational Publishers LLP trading as BBC Active
Edinburgh Gate
Harlow
Essex CM20 2JE
England

First published in 2005
This edition published in 2006

ISBN: 1406610232

Commissioning Editor: Emma Shackleton
Copyeditor: Florence Hamilton
Project Editor: Mari Roberts
Designer: Annette Peppis
Mind Maps ands Illustrations: Alan Burton
Production Controller: Man Fai Lau

Set in Frutiger
Printed and bound by Ashford Colour Press, UK

The Publisher's policy is to use paper manufactured from sustainable forests.

*It is not the strongest of the species who survive,
not the most intelligent,
but those who are the most adaptive to change.*

Charles Darwin

Contents

Acknowledgements

I would like to thank the following teams who have embraced change (and a lot more!) in helping me to complete this book:

Home team Caroline Shott, my Literary Manager, whose inspiration gave rise to this new BBC initiative; Lesley Bias, my Personal Assistant and 'Manuscript Manager', whose flying fingers typed the text; to my mother, Jean Buzan for her continuing and superb editorial feedback; to Vanda North, Founder and Head of Buzan Centres worldwide for her many 'all-nighters' staying up to give both feedback and inspiration for *Embracing Change*, to Sarah Sutton for her monumental work in bringing this text to fruition; to David Burt, Chairman of The Buzan Group, for his inspiration, input and deep support, and to Alan Matcham for bringing the principles described in this book into the workplace at Oracle.

Support team I would like also to give my appreciation to my extended team for their continuing help, feedback, stories and support.

My BBC team I want to thank especially my Commissioning Editor, Emma Shackleton for her diligence, creativity and professionalism in making sure that *Embracing Change* would be an extremely healthy and robust baby. Thanks also to Tracey Smith, Mari Roberts and Florence Hamilton for their excellent editing; to Rupert Gavin, Head of BBC Worldwide, for his support of this project; to Jennie Allen (Director of Communication, BBC Worldwide) and Sara Wikner for their many years of marketing and personal support; to Alix Tidmarsh and Amanda Hill for helping move forward so inspirationally the 'Buzan Brand'; to my Design Team, Annette Peppis and Alan Burton; and to Chris Weller, Head of BBC Books, 'Mon Oncle' for fielding this superb team.

Also, thanks go to: Eileen Campbell, John, Lois and Richard Sutton, Keith King, Nichola Vickers, Sue Hook, Jill Pearce, Bob Cox, Fiona Bradbeer & Steve Clancey, Mark Allen of Allen & York, and Sensei Paul Taylor.

*The universe is change;
our life is what our
thoughts make it.*

Marcus Aurelius Antoninus

Introduction

❏ About this book

❏ Using Change Mind Maps

❏ Why you owe it to yourself

Change is a feature of our lives from the moment of conception until the moment we die – and perhaps beyond. Change is happening all around us – literally, throughout every millisecond of our lives. Your entire mind–body system is designed not only to deal with change, but to thrive on it.

Embracing Change has been written to help you to understand the concept of change and yourself as an agent of change – to develop belief in your ability to live with and manage the effects of change, whatever the circumstances. You are a Change Thinker and Change Maker, with unique gifts and the ability to transform your own future and to make a positive impact on the world.

Embracing Change has been designed to enable you to identify your goals and to banish fears and false beliefs so that you can develop to your full potential and embrace the change offered in any situation.

Whatever your experiences to date, you have the strength and ability consciously to change the way you think, to break free of past patterns and embrace change as a natural part of that great experience called Life. *Embracing Change* will guide you through the process of recognizing who you truly are, who you want to be, and what you want to achieve.

On a practical level this book has been designed to provide you with a full range of **Tools for Personal Transformation**, which have been distilled from my courses and from the experiences of millions of readers and Change Makers around the world. These can be applied, whatever your personal situation, to enable all periods of change in your life to be viewed as opportunities for personal development.

Throughout you will find quotations from World Class Change Makers, and Case Studies from those who have used Mind Maps® and other techniques to bring about positive change in their own lives. You will choose your own support network of personal Change Masters to refer to and inspire you through your periods of change and will also find Attitude Check Points in the form of Buzan's Change Thinking Quotient, to keep you upbeat and on track.

By the time you have read this book you will have a clearer understanding of:

Change – What it is and how it affects us.

Self-perception – Understanding yourself as a Change Thinker and Change Maker: your attitude to change, how you see yourself, how others see you, your vision of the future, and how to release your true potential.

How to embrace change – Using Buzan's Tools for Transformation.

Life-planning – How to manage yourself during times of change: to choose the life you want to lead and take steps to achieve it.

To get the most from these tools you need only to use the single greatest *personal* tool for transformation ever created – Your Amazing BRAIN.

▨ Your attitude to change

How well do you know yourself? Do you see yourself as someone who is laid back and goes with the flow? Are you a 'control freak' who has always to know down to the last detail what is going to happen? Do you take care to plan things in advance? How do you cope in a crisis? Do you show anger? Nervousness? How well do you operate under pressure? How well do you cope with the unexpected? Do you see it as a challenge and meet it with a sense of enjoyment? Or is it an irritation, an obstacle sent to try you? When the chips are down – do you have a sense of humour, or do you feel only the need to be serious?

Throughout *Embracing Change*, I will show you just how powerful you are, how great is your personal influence and how all change can be transformed into a force of positive energy. Most importantly I will show you how to use your mind to a greater capacity, as an extraordinary tool for learning new skills, for recognizing – and releasing – your innermost thoughts, dreams and ambitions.

Take the change challenge

Change Challenges come in different forms. What is the Goal you want to plan and prepare for?

- Are you about to start a new school/ career/ job?
- Are you weighing up the pros and cons of starting a business?
- Have you a Vision of moving/ renovating a house?
- Will you shortly be getting married?
- Are you expecting or planning for a baby?
- Do you have considerations regarding becoming a step-parent?
- Do you anticipate new responsibilities following a promotion?

■ Are you dealing with the challenges of personal success or public recognition?

Or are you:

■ facing redundancy?
■ with a loved one who is destroying him or herself through alcohol/ drug abuse?
■ looking after a sick baby/ child/ parent?
■ facing personal anguish due to abandonment, divorce or bereavement?
■ supporting your partner through a period of personal difficulty?
■ faced with overwhelming financial problems?
■ broke/ overweight/ unfit/ depressed?
■ elderly, suffering from illness, or physically weaker than you used to be?

Some changes are exhilarating and sought-after, others may be anticipated with dread and in general avoided. We respond to every situation in life with an emotional response: 'This is how I am feeling', and a logical response: 'These are the facts'. We may be more aware of one response than the other, but in order to bring about constructive change it is important to embrace both these aspects of our thinking, to understand our true responses and determine our future actions.

If your motivation to read this book comes from an impending or recent change in your own life, take a moment to complete the following Change Mind Maps. These can be used as a first base in identifying your current state of mind.

What's Happening?

Change Mind Map: 1. Your situation

Place a key word on each line as you think of your current change situation.

How Do You Feel About It?

Change Mind Map: 2. Your feelings

Place a key word (or image) on each line as you capture all your feelings – the obvious ones *and* those beneath the surface.

Are you experiencing positive or negative feelings or a mixture of both? Really let rip, and get rid of the initial blast of emotions. Once you know how you feel about the situation, you can start to look objectively at the facts. If you suddenly think of something to add later, just add it. If you need more lines on your Change Mind Map – just add them!

What Do You Think About It?

Change Mind Map: 3. The facts – Where? Who? Why? What? How? When?

In the centre name the chief cause of change. Put FACTS only to each of the questions. If you are not sure whether it is a fact, add a ? or a !

It often seems, when Change comes, as if there is more than one situation going on at the same time. If you discover there is more than one set of facts emerging, create an additional Change Map.

Now PAUSE – and keep your Change Mind Maps. We will revisit them in Chapter 6. They are an exact reflection of how you are *thinking* at this moment; they will form the basis of your first Mind Map later in the book (see p.104).

You may be surprised that the words you have chosen to describe a traditionally positive change (e.g. captaining the soccer team, getting married, gaining a promotion, having a baby) include elements of fear and apprehension, whereas an enforced change, often assumed to be negative (e.g. the end of a relationship, being made redundant), may on some level show feelings of relief or have the potential to become a positive or liberating experience.

A 'positive' change such as a promotion or the purchase of a new house is usually seen as a time for congratulation, as a new beginning, whereas bereavement or a financial loss is termed a 'crisis' and is seen as a negative change, or an ending. In fact, these are two sides of the same coin. Both require us to enter a state of change. Both require detachment from the past before embracing the future. Both will result in peaks, troughs and vital plateaus as we assimilate knowledge, experience and gain the confidence to move forward.

The following chapters will focus more deeply on your situation and help you to bring about the changes that you want to or need to make.

If you are facing a major crisis at this moment, the Buzan Tools for Transformation will enable you to change your perception, to focus on the opportunity instead of the problem, and to find the POSITIVE in the most negative of situations.

If you are planning to launch your Big Idea, the Buzan Tools and techniques for managing change will keep you focused, motivated and right on track to become the best you can possibly be.

■ Your next steps

From this point onwards you will be encouraged to focus on the possible, to recognize your achievements and your abilities; and, when you are ready, to push back your personal and creative boundaries by making use of the practical exercises that are included here.

You may well be thinking that you already know who you are and what you really need to do – and on one level you would be right. But the gap between thought and deed can take a long time. Making the move from passive knowledge to affirmative action is the first BIG step.

In our busy, modern lives we do so much by remote control: our 'couch potato' minds spend a lot of time 'channel hopping' and not enough time focusing on seeing the main programme through from start to finish, including the difficult bits. *Embracing Change* will enable you to plan your future so that you are better motivated to concentrate on those things that are related to your goals, and are able to 'video record' those aspects you need to revisit and learn from.

We spend so much time putting energy into our work, our friends, our families, our worries, that we are familiar with only a very small part of ourselves, and hence may have a rigid view of our potential. We are like icebergs in this respect – only a fraction of what we are capable of is visible either to ourselves or others.

With this in mind, I encourage you to use this book as a catalyst for positive change. Free yourself of any rigid ideas you might hold about who you are and what you can achieve, because in doing so you will be pre-judging yourself. Instead, open yourself up to the potential of your infinite capabilities and talents. Whatever kind of change you are facing as you read this book, you have the strength, the ability and the mind power to face it and recreate it on your own terms.

A time of change is a time of personal transformation and you deserve to take part consciously in such an experience. So enjoy the exploration – you will surprise yourself. You owe it to yourself to see how amazing you really are.

■ You are the captain of your spaceship

You are like a captain of a spaceship in the universe, a spaceship made up of your mind and your body and driven by your unique energy and enthusiasm. There are billions of galaxies, and multiple trillions of stars and planets for you to explore. You can go absolutely anywhere you please! But first – you've got to learn to pilot that spaceship, or risk crashing on the nearest planet, or being pulled back into the earth's orbit, entrapped by gravitational pull before you've even learned to fly.

PART ONE

What is change?

Nothing in the entire universe ever perishes, believe me, but things vary, and adopt a new form. The phrase 'being born' is used for beginning to be something different from what one was before, while 'dying' means ceasing to be the same. Though this thing may pass into that, and that into this, yet the sum of things remains unchanged.

Ovid, *Metamorphoses*

Chapter 1
The nature of change

❏ What is change?

❏ We are all Change Thinkers and Change Makers

❏ The river conundrum

The dictionary definition of **Change** is: *'To alter or make different: to put or give for another: to pass from one state to another: to exchange.'*

How exciting, how liberating, and – sometimes – how terrifying. Whether we like it or not, we are in a constant state of change, as is our society, our environment, our planet, and the universe itself. As you sit reading this book, your body is changing, drawing upon nutrients from the food you have eaten, and your mind is actively developing: interpreting and assimilating the words on the page, and forming a view in line with your own requirements. With every word your eyes take in your brain is changing. The brain with which you are reading at this second will be different in the next second and will continue to change every second for the rest of your life.

Even as you sleep your cells are regenerating. You are no longer exactly who you were yesterday; you are in the process of becoming who you will be tomorrow. You cannot halt change no matter how much you resist it. From the moment of conception each of us is growing and ageing.

This organic and evolutionary process means that we have infinite opportunities to improve who we are!

Think how impressive is the ability of the natural world to transform itself when under threat – from the effects of pollution, deforestation and other influences – into something that will survive and is ever more beautiful. Nature offers constant visual evidence that change can be an enhancing and transformative process.

This applies to people too. We have an infinite capacity for growth and change. Ironically, it is often when we feel stuck or fearful that we have the greatest capacity to 'dig deep' and transform, even though we may feel as if we have lost our way or no longer know who we are.

Organic change is a powerful process: quiet, gradual and rhythmic. We barely and rarely notice it. It is only when we are presented with unexpected, enforced or sudden change that we become conscious of our changing state. If we have chosen the change we may feel exhilarated and excited by the prospect. If we feel more acted upon than acting, we may become fearful, anxious or feel severely threatened at our temporary loss of control.

Embracing Change will explore the wonderful truth that each of us is a unique agent for change. We are all Change Thinkers and Change Makers with ideas and behaviours that we can choose to use positively or negatively to influence our futures.

The Change Thinker is the person who is armed with all the knowledge of how to deal with change, and has the techniques and tools with which to manage the change or bring about change in the ways desired.

The Change Maker is a change thinker who has applied change-thinking techniques to taking steps towards achieving a vision or goal. Change Makers have many characteristics of the entrepreneur, combining creative thinking, focus and passion with a healthy disregard for conformity in order to achieve their vision and thereby bring about real change in their lives – and, by implication, in the world.

Embracing Change will provide you with the tools you need to achieve change in a positive, life-enhancing way. The techniques will enable you to become a Change Thinker and Change Maker, with the ability to transform *any* perceived problem into a force for positive change.

◼ You think therefore you change

Every time you think, you change. You change the electrical impulses in your brain and you change the probability of what your next thought will be. So every thought you have, every fantasy you have, every fear you have, every emotional reaction you have changes the probability of what your next thoughts, emotions and reactions will be.

Child of Change

Child of the changeling
Stars
Born into
    Change
Born of
    Change
Born to
    Change
You Can:
You Are:

Change
Yourself

You live and play in the playground of change for your entire life, and the choice that you have is whether you are going to enjoy it or whether you are going to get overwhelmed. It really is that stark. Therefore your knowledge of what change is and your attitude towards it are things that are going to determine your future and in large part the future of people around you.

In a sense you are like a surf rider surfing a giant wave of change. You perceive change, and then stabilize yourself within that change. You are wholly yourself within it, while also being carried by it.

■ The surf rider

As a surf rider you learn to monitor the changes in the power and the rhythms of the waves. Years of experience and determination and learning on smaller waves increase experience and the hunger to ride a *giant* wave.

First you need the motivation to learn to surf – to battle out to sea, pushing against the power and weight of the waves against your body. The sea spray entering your mouth and your nostrils adds to the tension and the anticipation as you watch and FEEL the changing rhythm of the ocean – waiting for the rush of energy *before* the wave that determines whether or not it is time for you to go.

If you get the timing right, as a giant wave approaches you will ensure you are in position on your surfboard, paddling ahead of that wave, ahead of that oncoming power-source of energy – which could grow to become 20 metres high and dwarf you. Your aim will be to ride the power of the wave and become a part of it. If you get it right, it will hurtle along, and you will travel for miles, literally riding the energy of that wave to your total enjoyment, advantage and ecstasy.

If you get the timing wrong, if you end up on top of the wave, or just beneath its crest, instead of riding the positive energy of the wave you will experience its negative power. The wave will break. The wave will break *on you* – and below you there will be space, sand or rocks. All the energy of that wave, that same wave, carrying the same you, on the same surfboard, instead of transporting you to new heights, will smash you into the ground. You will have nowhere to go other than down. You will be bruised and grazed – and your ego severely dented.

The only difference in this two-part scenario is that one of you went *with* the energy of the oncoming wave, literally *with* the flow of the wave, to become part of it. The other one didn't. The difference is absolute.

Our relationship with life-changes is similar. Everything has its moment. If we miss that moment, then we may bob around listlessly for a while, or risk being dumped unceremoniously on 'the beach of life'.

Just as a wave keeps the same form for hundreds of miles and BUILDS and BUILDS and BUILDS and BUILDS and BUILDS ... so, too, you build and progress in knowledge. As you learn, so you learn to go *with* the process and become at one with the waves until, at a certain critical and cataclysmic stage you change; you transform. Each time you learn to go with a learning curve, you are personally transformed, absorbing the maximum level of information possible at that level. The euphoria leads to an increase in self-confidence and self-knowledge and the motivation to begin to become a part of the next learning curve, ready to learn and experience anything.

If you learn how to ride the waves of change, learn how literally to use *your* self-belief and energy to go *consciously* with the flow of change, then you will be advantaged. If you don't – change has the capacity to be highly destructive, and the adjustment can be a much longer and harder learning curve.

Look at another scenario. If you are swimming in a flowing river and you are trying to get to a fixed point on the shore but the tide is taking you away from that point, it becomes very dangerous to swim against the tide. It is far better to go *with* the tide at an angle that will take you to a different point on the shore – further up. Why? Because the amount of energy it will take to swim against the tide and the weight of the water will exhaust you, and it will take a lot, *lot* longer to reach your destination (if you get there at all). If you go *with* the energy of the river and angle yourself towards the shore, you may miss your initial target, but you can walk back to the place you were trying to get to.

The long way is often the shorter way.

■ The change paradox

Change is a paradox because we are in a constant state of change and, although the pace may change – it may accelerate, plateau, and then accelerate again – yet we appear to remain the same from moment to moment.

Changing 'Change'

Every time I write
Or read
The word 'Change'
The word 'Change'
Changes

Are you
'Change'
The only word
That is the essence
Of itself?

Nature too is capable of catastrophic and catalytic change. In general the organic progression is an astonishing yet gradual and subtle process. Consider the way that the buds and blossoms of spring transform into the leaves of summer and the fruits of autumn in ways that are both clearly visible and yet so gradual that unless you are a gardener or horticulturist, the day-to-day changes go largely undetected. Each stage of growth is perfection in its own right and exquisite preparation for the next manifestation.

In the same way, it is only over an extended period of time that we notice the impact of our thousand upon thousand of thoughts on our behaviour, or the changes that the movement of a multitude of molecules has on our internal and external environments.

We are an intrinsic part of the cycles of nature, experiencing through our senses the unique beauty of each new dawn at the break of every day, responding to the ever-changing impact of the weather, appreciating the fanfare of many styles of sunset before the multicoloured darkness that we call night. Organic growth, the cycles of nature and cataclysmic changes in the energies of the Earth and indeed the universe offer important metaphors for our own relationship with change that will be explored throughout the book.

All *is* change
You *are* change

To illustrate this further I would like to tell you a story about Change. The story takes place at the beginning of the last century ...

■ A tale of change

Beneath the gleaming spires of the world-renowned Oxford University in England, there resided a Professor of Logic called Dr Arbuthnot Thwaite. An academic of some stature, he was an incisive intellectual who had developed a
formidable reputation for being undefeated in debate. His reputation was a
considerable source of pride to him, and he took comfort from the knowledge
that his colleagues and students must hold him in great esteem as a result. His
world was one of intellectual rigour and self-discipline. He had no doubt that
in debate he was more than a match for anyone.

Imagine his consternation therefore when he heard that in Kyoto, Japan,
there resided a Zen Master by the name of Hyakawa San, who also had a formidable reputation for being undefeated in debate.

Being a stalwart fellow of competitive spirit, Professor Arbuthnot
Thwaite found out where Hyakawa San, was next presenting. As circumstance
would have it, he was scheduled to appear at an International Philosophical
Conference, to be hosted within an ancient Samurai palace in Kyoto, the very
next month. Such was Arbuthnot Thwaite's reputation that he was able to
arrange to be invited to present at the conference also.

He arrived in Japan in good humour, unbowed by his long flight, and
after he had checked in to his hotel room, went immediately to the conference
reception area to enquire the whereabouts of Hyakawa San. The organizers
explained that Hyakawa San was outside meditating by the side of a river that
ran through the palace grounds.

Seemingly oblivious to his tranquil and elegant surroundings, Arbuthnot
Thwaite strode in determined fashion out into the grounds, past the rustling
willow trees, unaware of the heady scent of the camellias, deaf to the song of
the boundless songbirds, until he saw Hyakawa San sitting cross-legged
gazing into the river.

Arbuthnot Thwaite's spirits soared, his confidence abundant. 'Excuse me,
sir!' proclaimed Arbuthnot Thwaite. 'Are you the famous Zen Master, Hyakawa
San, who is undefeated in debate?'

Hyakawa San looked up from his contemplations, his hands lying calmly
on his immaculate kimono, and smiled beatifically at Arbuthnot Thwaite. *'Hai!*
I am Hyakawa San. Undefeated in debate!'

'Excellent!' said Arbuthnot Thwaite. 'Please allow me to introduce myself:

I am Professor Arbuthnot Thwaite, Senior Don of Philosophy and Logic at Oxford University. I, too, remain undefeated in debate.'

Then, drawing himself up to his full height, Arbuthnot Thwaite said, 'Hyakawa San, I am so pleased to find you sitting by the side of this stream. It just so happens that I have prepared the introduction to a private debate that you and I might have (in confidence, of course) to see which one us would remain undefeated in a private competition.' He continued with earnest haste: 'Coincidentally, the question I have prepared for you concerns the river. Are you willing, now, to engage me in this debate?'

'I would be delighted!' said Hyakawa San, with a respectful bow and a clear gaze.

Crouching down by the side of Hyakawa San, like a hunter about to catch its prey, and with a gleam in his eye, Professor Arbuthnot Thwaite released the defining question: 'My dear Hyakawa San, this is my question: *Is it possible to step into the same river twice?*'

Hyakawa San turned his head away from Arbuthnot Thwaite, stared into the river and remained silent for five or so minutes.

After this time, impatient for his victory, Professor Arbuthnot Thwaite said, 'Come, come, Hyakawa San, enough of this prevarication, it's time for your answer.'

Hyakawa San slowly turned and looked up with sadness in his face. 'Ahhh,' he sighed, 'is it possible, my esteemed opponent, that you do not know that it is impossible to step into the same river *once*?'

Draw your own conclusions …

Why is it impossible to step into the same river once? Take time to consider this conundrum, for it illustrates the essence of change and what our lives are all about.

■ The answer

The truth is that the river is in constant change, and it has changed its form even before your big toe breaks the surface of the water. In every second that passes, billions of molecules and atoms of water will pass by you. The light is changing constantly because each tiny ripple on the river's surface will reflect the sun's rays in completely different directions; the myriad living creatures that were in one position as you were about to step in the river will be in another position by the time you have both feet on the floor of the river bed. The river bed is no longer the river bed that was there while you stood at the bank. It will have changed in billion-fold ways.

According to Hyakawa San (and your author) it is therefore impossible to step into the 'same' river even once. Why? Because the river, like the stream of your thoughts, the flow of your bloodstream and immune system, is in a constant state of flux and change. The river is therefore *not* the 'same' river. With each second that passes, you are seeing *many* different rivers. Just as, in each second that passes, your life changes.

To be a Change Thinker you need to embrace this concept, and to understand that everything you have experienced to date has led to this moment, and that each moment impacts on the future – your future, the future of those around you, and by implication the future of those you have never, and will never, meet.

Some men see things as they are and say, 'Why?' I dream of things that never were and say, 'Why not?'

George Bernard Shaw

Chapter 2
Your unique change-management system

❏ The extraordinary power of your brain

❏ Your sensory change agents

❏ Take action for physical health

In order to manage yourself effectively you need to understand the fundamental principles of your unique management system: your ever-changing brain and body. As well as understanding what your brain and body actually are and how they function, let me show you how to release their amazing and unique capabilities. The nature of change and the ways in which our system is embraced by change will then become ever clearer and infinitely more powerful.

Each of us is an individual and we each look physically different. We are far more different on the inside, however, than on the outside, with a literally infinite differentiation between us as human beings. Whereas externally we have generally similar structures, internally our thoughts are private and unique universes.

Your body is an extraordinary creation that provides a perfect example of the paradox that is change. Your breath, your blood, your cells are functioning constantly to ensure that your whole body is kept in homeostasis. The body maintains its internal equilibrium by adjusting its physiological processes. Just as, using our river metaphor, if you are swimming in a river and you want to stay in the same position, you would have to move in order to stay still.

You can only remain constant by changing.
You can only stay where you are by moving.

So, in a very physical way, you, via your body, embrace change during every moment, every second, every millisecond, every nanosecond, of every hour of every day or every week, month, year, decade of your life.

■ Your mind is a universe

We are each exposed to a multiplicity of influences, but each mind is a universe unto itself. The universe inside your head is uniquely yours and it is also an infinite universe; you have total and individual ownership of the knowledge within it.

The August 2003 issue of *New Scientist* focused exclusively on the brain and stated boldly on the front cover that it was featuring 'A brave new vision of your brain: **No Limits**'. Just a few months earlier they featured a picture of a brain with a universe inside it with the heading 'The Universe inside Your Head'. This means You. *You* were featured on the front cover of that magazine.

You have No Limits. *You* have a universe inside *your* head.

It is important to understand this, to understand the context in which you exist and in which you are working, because you are truly amazing; you can achieve absolutely anything you choose to achieve.

Your brain – the ultimate change agent

The Brain – is wider than the sky –
For – put them side by side –
The one the other will contain
With ease –
Emily Dickinson, 'Part One: Life CXVII'

The power of the human brain is extraordinary. Each brain contains well over one million million brain cells (neurons), that is, well over 1,000,000,000,000 brain cells. Each of these powerful knowledge generators and managers combined contains more information than can be held in all the libraries in the world. Its memory capacity is infinite and our ability to change and grow is also infinite. Amazingly, however, we have known that the brain is the main driver for our thoughts and actions for only 500 years, and 95 per cent of everything we *know* about the brain has been discovered in the last ten years. How much more we have to learn! The twenty-first century has already been designated 'The Century of Intellectual Capital and Innovation' by President Vincente Fox of Mexico, for good reason.

When considering how to cope with the changes in our lives the most important facts to understand about the brain are that: *the brain is self-creating*, and *the brain is truth-seeking*.

The brain is self-creating

The brain is programmed to think in a 'synergetic' fashion – meaning that whatever quality of information you put into your brain, whether positive or negative, it will multiply that information to an infinite degree. You reprogramme your brain with every thought and every instruction you give it. That is why it is vitally important to ensure that you are feeding your brain with constructive, positive, appropriate messages, in order to nurture positive, dynamic change.

■ The brain is truth-seeking

The brain is pre-programmed to be knowledge-seeking, truth-seeking, successful in whatever you programme it to do, and persistent. Whatever you programme your brain to do – negative or positive – it will ensure that you do it to the best of your ability. All you need to do is:

**Plant the seeds of Positive Thought
and you will reap a harvest of Positive Change.**

■ The Breath of Life

In all spiritual traditions, the Breath of Life is linked to the concept of Spirit. The origin of the meaning of the word Spirit is breath, and quite literally breath is what gives us life. Breath is our life force; it is also at the very *root* of change.

Breath is at the root of change.

You breathe. You inhale. You exhale. As you do so you are changing the content and quality of the energy systems in your body. You are oxygenating your blood; you are keeping your heart muscle nourished ensuring that your brain is kept well supplied and functioning to its optimum capacity at that moment. Every time your heart beats, it is changing the blood throughout every part of your many tens of thousands of miles of blood vessels. Each one of your organs is being replenished and refreshed – and is in a constant state of change – in order to keep you alive.

**You embrace change
Change embraces you.**

Our physical beings are also embraced by changes that influence the internal physiology, and our intellectual and sensual responses. We are embraced by change through the vehicle of our extraordinary senses.

Your sensory change agents

Man has no body distinct from his soul; for that called body is a portion of soul discerned by the five senses, the chief inlets of soul in this age.
William Blake

You have within your body an extraordinary army of sensory change agents which are in a constant state of transformation; which are more sophisticated than the most technologically advanced gadgetry; which update their memory automatically every time you 'key in' additional data through your behaviour and your experiences; which provide you with sophisticated sensory radar to interpret your ever-changing world. Your senses are the brain's tools for making associations, links and connections between the kinds of information you are gathering from your life's experiences, in order to experience, interpret, understand and bring about change.

Sensory change agent: sound

Consider your hearing. The transmission and interpretation of sound is based entirely on change. When someone speaks, or plays music, or slams a car door, that person's voice, that mellow sound, that jarring noise, moves the molecules of the air in the form of sound waves. The sound waves change the surface contact and the rhythm of the receptor parts of that phenomenal musical instrument we rather dully call an ear. You change your interpretation of the world with every sound you hear.

Sensory change agent: sight

Your eye is monitoring constantly the fabulous universal changes that go on around us trillion-fold, at a rate of 186,000 miles per second, in a form we call light. All light is movement, the changing movement of energy, which the eye then reads and interprets via your brain using your sense of sight. In this way you simultaneously experience rapid change while momentarily remaining in one place. Changes in the receptors of the eye transmit the image to your visual cortex, enabling you to understand what you see and make sense spatially of where you are. You then have a choice – do you move or do you stay put?

■ Sensory change agent: smell

Your nose contains a myriad of sensory receptors ready to interpret the subtle and not so subtle meaning of the trillions of molecules that change form and enter your nostrils as a range of smells. Amazingly, as you breathe and change the energy levels in your body, so your olfactory system simultaneously checks the changing smells in the environment. The ability to read change via your nose is so effective that you are able to tell instantly whether you are experiencing the aroma of a beautiful flowery perfume or whether you're in imminent danger of being poisoned by a dangerous substance. Additionally, your sense of smell has a very particular effect on your memory and will provide instant recall of moments or people associated with particular scents as far back as childhood.

■ Sensory change agent: taste

Consider for a moment your marvellous sense of taste and your taste buds. You have an infinite capacity to detect subtle differences in flavour, which has an influence extending far beyond the taste of the food or your basic need to keep your body alive. Your sense of taste feeds your sensual appetites and connects you to others, to other cultures, to your past, and to the growing of food itself.

Taste is a function of a direct result of change. When your body is in need of nutrients, your biochemical warning system goes into action – to let your body know that it needs certain forms of food. Your infinitely subtle chemical laboratory (your mouth!) can distinguish between millions of different substances, and recognizes more or less instantaneously whether they are good for you or should be expelled immediately. Your changing appetite for food tells you not only when you need to eat, in order to feed the nutritional needs of your ever-changing body, it also tells you when you are replete.

Your mouth is itself the ultimate change agent. Most tasting comes about as a direct result of mastication – changing the consistency of your food – thereby allowing your digestive system to distinguish the desirable from the undesirable and ingest (or excrete) accordingly.

You may have noticed that very young children, when eating a food that is known to them but unknown to a companion, may transfix their companion with their eyes and open their mouths when chewing the food. This basic and instinctive behaviour (commonly misconstrued as *mis*behaviour) shows not only the process of change taking place (literally!) but also demonstrates that 'this food is safe for consumption'.

One of the fastest growing hobbies in the world is cooking. Everyone – every mum, every dad, every kid, every chef – who ever prepares a meal, is an agent of change. For what is cooking and the preparation of food other than directing the change of the state of the ingredients to be eaten in a way that makes them presentable and palatable to the senses?

Taste is used as an active agent of positive change in the forming of family, social and business relationships. The romantic dinner, the celebratory festive meal, the business breakfast, the business lunch – where food is often the catalytic centrepiece – are almost always seen as positive occasions.

■ Sensory change agent: touch

The skin is the largest organ of the body and the ultimate monitor and agent of change. It envelops the whole body and embraces us, literally, with constant sensual change. We all know from personal experience that the skin is capable of responding very fast, with extraordinary sensitivity and transformation, to the slightest touch or sensation. Our sense of touch connects us to our outer world through sensations which say this is hot, cold, soft, silky, rough, sharp, metallic, smooth and prompt a multiplicity of other reactions. The sense of touch is both immensely powerful and immediately transformative. Contact with the skin sends urgent messages to the brain alerting it to pain, pleasure, fear or delight and enables us to change our responses to whatever or whomever it is we are touching or being touched by.

To monitor and adapt to change your skin has tens of millions of sensors that are, microsecond by microsecond, monitoring the constant changes in temperature, texture, air quality, sound and, amazingly, smell and light as well, in order to keep your body in a state of general equilibrium. As a result of the information your skin receives, you will make minute-to-major adjustments in your position as your brain reacts to the constant and ever-changing stream of information it receives.

Your senses allow you to experience the outer world via the changes that occur both in the molecules that transmit those messages to your body, and also via the neurological and sensory changes that take place within your body in order to transmit the messages to your brain. You are capable of experiencing all kinds of wonderful things – in your constant state of growth and change.

Why do you change position? Because you want to be in a position that is more acceptable to you, more advantageous to you, more comfortable for you; and because you would endanger your health if you did not. Your muscles would begin to twitch, your blood-flow would slow and would begin to pool in your limbs, and your body would stagnate. Compare the difference in the skin tone between an active person and an inactive person. Bright eyes and a healthy glow are the result of keeping the blood pumping and oxygenated through constant and healthy physical movement.

■ Using all your senses
One of the reasons we remember times that we have spent with close friends is because when we are with our friends we are usually eating, listening, conversing, looking with wide-open pupils, touching or moving in some way. We are likely to be using all our senses and our responses are heightened.

■ Your body-balance barometer: the immune system
The immune system is your master change manager and your body-balance barometer. A healthy immune system appears to be unchanging. It can be seen as one of the ultimate metaphors for you the individual, as an object of constant change in yourself, operating to keep yourself both constant and

changing. It is another example of the change paradox: a giant change system designed to help you monitor change by keeping you unchanging.

The immune system is comprised of a galactically large, highly effective army of biological change agents, specifically designed to keep you in homoeostasis and to keep all your change processes constant – monitoring all internal and external change. Sensual stimuli maintain a constant flow of information to the brain, enabling it to monitor the change that is going on around you.

If you feel unaware of your immune system, it is because you are living with the benefits of it. You are likely to be aware instead that you are physically very healthy, or feel energetic and positive about your life. The immune system is a perfect barometer for telling whether your Mind–Body system is in balance and whether or not you are a competent change manager. When your body is healthy and your life is in balance your immune system will be naturally vigorous and robust, enabling you to feel 'alive' to life and its possibilities.

■ Sensory change agent: kinaesthetic

The constant state of change is demonstrated physically by the body's frequent desire to move and its ability to know where it is in space and, to some extent, time. As anyone who has studied the Alexander Technique will tell you, even when standing upright and apparently still, our bodies will sway. Witness policemen or soldiers who are on guard duty; their constant change of position is essential in order to stay upright, even when essentially standing still.

When the immune system becomes out of balance, your health is at risk. You may feel seriously fatigued, develop unfamiliar allergies, food intolerance or become more susceptible to immune-deficient conditions such as colds, stomach upsets, flu, asthma or eczema.

Action point

If your immune system appears out of balance, PAY ATTENTION to what your body is telling you, as it means that you are becoming a poor change manager and need to nurture yourself. If your lack of balance continues, you are at risk of severe long-term physical or psychological health problems.

To maintain homoeostasis and optimum health, it is important to look after the extraordinary system that is your mind and body.

■ Physical health and fitness

Think of yourself as a perfect futuristic robot. If you were the commander of yourself as a robot and you wanted to function perfectly, what would you do? Would you make sure that your circuits were regularly checked, that your bodywork was clean, that your living conditions were not conducive to rusting, that your joints were well oiled and mechanics regularly serviced, upgraded and displayed to perfection? Of course you would.

I am here to tell you that you have so much more to offer than a futuristic robot. You are the commander of a unique operating system that is perfection incarnate. To operate maximally means quite simply that your body has to be kept well-maintained and healthy.

If you are unfit and your nourishment is poor, all your energy levels will slide. You will become stagnant: in the sense of becoming unmoving, unchanging, or changing towards becoming *more* unchanging! A body that is stagnant will eventually corrupt itself. It will disrupt the immune system, lose its ability to self-heal, will have no freedom of will, no ability to act to preserve its goal and its ability to change.

A healthy body is a body that is functioning to its maximum potential. It is a body that is taking in the appropriate amount of oxygen, with muscles that are toned, a heart and circulation system that are healthy, an immune system that is functioning at maximum efficiency. Your body is a giant massive universe of constant change. If that massive change system itself wants to bring about change, it *needs* to be functioning properly.

Action point

Even a small level of exercise can rejuvenate you – instantly! If you are feeling sluggish, perpetually tired or self-conscious about your weight, why not start treating your self to 20 minutes exercise a day? This can be as simple as taking a brisk power walk to post a letter. Once you've got the habit, and begin to feel better, you will be motivated to up the pace and keep on moving.

The good news is that the body is pre-programmed to heal. All you have to do is nourish it with regular, healthy exercise, balanced nutrition, plenty of fresh water and the restorative powers of plenty of sleep. Hmmmm ... how enjoyable, and how much easier than keeping a robot oiled and serviced!

Carefully watch your THOUGHTS,
for they become your WORDS.
Manage and watch your WORDS,
for they will become your ACTIONS.
Consider and judge your ACTIONS,
for they have become your HABITS.
Acknowledge and watch your HABITS,
for they shall become your VALUES.
Understand and embrace your VALUES,
for they become YOUR DESTINY.

Mahatma Gandhi

Chapter 3
Your attitude to change

❏ Introducing Buzan's Tools for Transformation

❏ Tools for Transformation:
   1. Your Change Thinking Quotient (CTQ)

❏ Questionnaire: what's your Attitude to Change?

There are many ways in which we can personally affect and manage the outcome of change. The Tools for Transformation used throughout this book include processes and techniques that have been designed to enable you to influence, in a positive and constructive way, your mighty, powerful, motivating, change-making Brain – the powerhouse from which all thoughts, feelings and decisions stem.

■ Introducing the Tools for Transformation

These change-management techniques have been developed over many years. They are used around the world at all levels, whether for running a home and family, for planning social events, or for achieving effective business management. They have been used to powerful effect in politics, in international business, in education, in sport and every aspect of human life.

Each technique will focus the way you think, and enhance your creative ability, your social behaviour, and your attitude to business. Used effectively in partnership these techniques will enable you to achieve optimum balance in life – in mind, body and spirit.

1. Your Change Thinking Quotient (CTQ)

At the centre of your self is your extraordinary brain, with the power to influence your attitude and therefore your feelings about an event or situation. Your attitude and your feelings are powerful predictors for the outcome of change. Do you either consciously or unconsciously see yourself as a victim of circumstance, or do you have the self-belief and the courage to approach each situation assuming that you will gain the best from the situation, that you will be a victor? Your Attitude is measured via your personal Change Thinking Quotient. Rather as the IQ test was devised as a measure of intelligence, so the CTQ has been devised as a measure of your current capacity for, and attitude to, the change in your life. (See pages 47–51.)

2. Vision and Focus

Vision and Focus are the two most important factors in ensuring that you bring about directed and proactive change.

If you arrive at a railway station and want to get on a train, you need to decide where you want to go to before you buy your ticket. You may decide to stop off at other places en route, but the chances are, having bought that ticket, you will be motivated to stay on track and reach your ultimate destination. Buying a ticket for the wrong place will lead you to interesting new territory, but will distract from helping you to reach your original goal.

The same is true in life. If you do not know where you are headed, you will not know where you are going, and nor will you know when you have arrived. I will show you how to refocus on your future and enhance your creativity in order to clarify your vision. (See Chapter 4.)

3. TEFCAS

TEFCAS is the acronym for the change process by which you progress and learn throughout life. It stands for:

T   Try

E   Event

F   Feedback

C   Check

A   Adjust

S   Success

It is the process by which we act, react and monitor change. It is not a psychological theory; it is a scientific process each of us is bound to follow. We have no choice. We do have a choice in whether we follow the process consciously, however, so that we are in a constant state of learning and adjustment. (See Chapter 5.)

4. Mind Maps

Mind Maps are the method by which we reflect upon and refine our thoughts and emotions to give life to our Goals and Vision. To enable you to release your personal brain power I will introduce the concepts of **Radiant Thinking** and **Mind Mapping**. (See Chapter 6.)

5. Meta-Positive Thinking

Whether you have a positive or negative approach to change, whether you see yourself as a victor or a victim in a given situation can be transformed or enhanced by applying Meta-Positive Thinking to everything that you think, do or say. This is not a 'Pollyanna' approach but rather the conscious choice to face the situation head-on, no matter how painful or challenging, and to look positively at what can be done and what *can* be changed. (See Chapter 7.)

6. Your Change Masters

In the words of John Donne, 'No man is an island, entire of itself', and throughout our lives we need to consult and be inspired by role models and mentors – our personal agents for change. It is vitally important in life to know Change Thinkers who can help us to manage our personal change process and to achieve our goals. On page 148 I introduce thirteen iconic Change Masters and explain how their values, tenacity, courage and success can influence our own. (See Chapter 8.)

7. Keeping a Change Journal

It is vital to our health and our survival that we achieve Life Balance as a part of our process of ongoing change. Many of the greatest creative minds in history kept notebooks and diaries over many years. Keeping a Change Journal will ensure that you not only achieve your aim, but that you can also chart the path that tells you how far you have come. (See Chapter 9.)

How you think about change

If you want evidence of the ability of your human brain to bring about change, just look around you, wherever you are at the moment. Look at every single item in your immediate environment, and ask yourself the following questions:

- Was that item, whether tiny or gigantic, once non-existent?
- Did it come into existence as the result of a thought that wanted to bring about a change?

You will find that virtually everything you see once existed only as a thought.

It is thoughts (yours included) that bring about *all* the prime changes and products of life. If you can learn to control your thoughts well, you *will* bring about conscious change. Changes that you bring about will be for your own benefit, and the benefit of others. The Tools for Transformation that we will be exploring in *Embracing Change* will help you to realize your ambitions and to overcome your personal challenges, no matter how small, no matter how large, no matter how immediate or distant they seem at the moment.

How you feel about change

Our individual responses to change will be diverse and personal, but what is common to all responses is the fact that our *thoughts*, and therefore our *attitude* and *feelings* about the change and responses to it, are as important as the change itself.

Our feelings are the barometer, showing how external influences and learned responses are affecting our thoughts. They are the pressure gauge that measures our personal attitude and indicates whether we are approaching the changing climate of the situation in a way that is constructive or destructive.

At times our feelings can overwhelm us; we lose control and forget that we have the ability to influence the outcome of any situation. In fact, we each have the ability to influence our chosen futures because we each have at our disposal the most powerful and amazing of creations – the human brain. With the brain comes the ability to think – and ultimately to influence and CHOOSE the way we respond.

Remember – whether or not you decide to act, change will still take place.

To help you gain some objective feedback about your own attitude to change and the possibility of achieving personal success, take a few minutes to complete the following questionnaire. It has been designed as an Attitude Health Check to help you take stock when you are embarking on a new venture, to enable you to check your self-talk and adjust your attitude in order to stride towards success.

Buzan's Tools for Transformation

1. Your Change Thinking Quotient (CTQ)

The Change Thinking Quotient has been designed to give you a benchmark to measure your approach to change on a scale from victim of circumstance to complete Change Thinker and Change Maker.

The rest of my tools for change are designed to help you to release yourself from negative or self-limiting approaches to change, and so I encourage you to revisit this questionnaire from time to time to see how your thoughts are changing.

On a scale from 0 to10, rate yourself on the following statements. 0 = FALSE: the absolute bottom of the scale. 10 = TRUE: the absolute top of the scale.

There are no right or wrong answers. This questionnaire is designed solely as a mirror to show you how you think.

1. I have a clear vision of what I want to achieve in life
2. I find it hard to react positively if my plans are disrupted unexpectedly
3. I am confident that if I decide to do something, it will be accomplished
4. I often feel helpless
5. I enjoy the opportunity to tackle new tasks and challenges
6. I'm not very good at learning new things
7. I think in pictures
8. I often find that problems prevent me from taking action
9. I am not afraid to challenge the status quo
10. I often have to explain to people why things can't be done
11. I regularly plan ahead
12. I often rely on my gut feelings
13. I enjoy leading and inspiring others
14. I often find that I don't really care about the outcome of a situation
15. I am creative
16. I never have enough time to put my ideas into action
17. I regularly take holidays and break up my working day
18. I am tired of feeling broke
19. I enjoy working as part of a team
20. I am often prevented from doing things through fear or nervousness
21. I have a 'can do' attitude
22. I regularly tell myself not to be so stupid
23. I like my body

24. I dread the idea of getting older
25. I have a healthy and varied diet
26. I keep meaning to get fit
27. I take (and enjoy) regular exercise
28. I often feel that things in my life are not fair
29. I am a generally happy person
30. I feel trapped by my current situation

Once you have finished the questionnaire, add up the totals of the answers to the odd-numbered questions; then add up the totals of the answers to the even-numbered questions.

Odd-numbered questions   Even-numbered questions

_____   _____

The **odd-numbered** questions focus on whether you have **Positive** thoughts about change and your level of control within that change.

The **even-numbered** questions focus on whether you have **Negative** thoughts about change and your level of control within that change.

If the total for the odd-numbered questions is higher than the total for the even-numbered questions, then you are already a Change Thinker. The higher this total is, the more of a Change Thinker you are.

If your even-numbered answers total higher than your odd-numbered answers, the reverse is true. You may still be a Change Thinker, but you have some work to do on your negative thinking habits, and the chapters following will help you transform your approach.

Subtract the total for the even-numbered questions from the total for the odd-numbered questions. This is your CTQ. It will be a positive or a negative number.

The higher the odd-numbered total and the greater the positive difference between the totals, the more likely you are to be a Change Maker as well as a Change Thinker in approach, as the following examples show. Change Thinkers A, B and C work in the same marketing department. A is the divisional director, B is a technician, C is an administrator. Each agreed to complete the questionnaire above, but their results were significantly different.

A

Positive questions: 126
Negative questions: 45
Difference: 81 (Positive)

B

Positive questions: 79
Negative questions: 67
Difference: 12 (Positive)

C

Positive questions: 83
Negative questions: 148
Difference: 65 (Negative)

A   A's high positive total shows clearly that he is a positive Change Thinker. The significant positive difference between the negative and the positive total also suggests he has the attributes of a Change Maker. A person with this Change Profile takes responsibility for his or her actions and is not afraid to face or bring about change.

B   B's total is also more positive than negative and also shows the attributes of a positive Change Thinker. However, the relatively low totals and the small difference between the positive and negative totals suggests that negative thinking is also playing a part and preventing him from developing the positive attitude of a Change Maker. A person with this Change Profile is likely to go with the flow and be more reactive than proactive in his or her approach to change.

C   C's totals are more negative than positive but the positive score shows that this person is in fact more of a positive Change Thinker than B. The larger negative score suggests that there is low self-esteem at work here, but positive attention to this can transform C's attitude so that he is ready to become a positive Change Maker. A person with this Change Profile is likely to see him or herself as a victim of circumstance and to feel he or she has little control over life.

Your CTQ result

A group of individuals faced with the same change will each have a very different response to that change. Consider whether your result shows you to be feeling positive or negative about change at the moment. Mark your result on the 'Action Line' following:

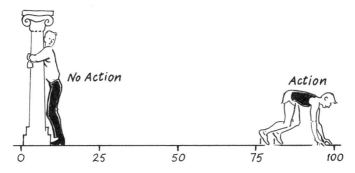

'0' is the worst Negative feeling and '100' is the best possible Positive feeling. Mark the line with your initials to show where you are now.

Use the questionnaire to revisit your Attitude every few days or months (depending on how long the change situation is taking) to see whether you are talking to yourself in a positive and encouraging way, or whether you are limiting the outcome by adopting a negative attitude. This in turn affects your self-esteem.

■ Managing high self-esteem

High self-esteem indicates that the mind and body are working in balance, that your brain is used to receiving messages that are positive and nurturing. You have every faith that your ideas are sound and that you have the capacity to achieve your goals. You are a Change Thinker by nature and a Change Maker by instinct. The techniques in this book will enable you to reach the very top of where you want to go. In Part 2 you will be introduced to the concept of META-POSITIVE THINKING, which will help to enhance your ability further.

In progressing towards achieving your ambitions you will benefit from the experience and support of your CHANGE MASTER GROUP (Chapter 8), who will encourage you to test your theories, ask searching questions and constantly review your progress to enable you to keep on track.

Your lack of familiarity with 'failure' may mean that you are hit extra hard when faced by a cataclysmic event that rocks your world or threatens your track record of personal success. For further information about this, review the material on Success on pages 83–4.

■ Transforming low self-esteem

If, in your low moments, you compare yourself unfavourably with others and reject the gifts you were born with, you will face the future with a sense of defeat and may feel like closing down, retreating, switching off from the world. If, however, you recognize that you are simply experiencing a short-term personal low, and that you need to pause to take stock, re-focus and re-motivate yourself, you will be able with practice to focus on your positive attributes, enabling you to face the future with a sense of empowerment.

Whatever kind of change you are planning or living through, the experience and your response to it will feel unique to you, and you alone. The good news is that low self-esteem can be transformed into positive self-esteem.

In every challenging and painful situation there are positive aspects to be found, no matter how distant the glimmers of light may appear to be. I am not saying that you should dismiss your feelings, or that you should pull yourself together – far from it. But if you focus carefully on finding the positive aspects and make plans towards a new goal, you will get through – with planning and patience, and one step at a time.

The important thing to realize is that whether or not you are able to approach the situation with positive heart and mind, change will still occur. The more you are able to embrace the process of change, the more likely you are to feel in control of the outcome.

Concentrate all your thoughts upon the work at hand. The sun's rays do not burn until brought to a focus.

Alexander Graham Bell

Chapter 4
Your vision of change

❑ Buzan's Tools for Transformation: 2. Vision and Focus

❑ Forms of change: natural, advised, anticipated and enforced

❑ How two rivers meet and stabilize

❑ Transformation, and the phases of change

Have you ever stopped to consider your own immense capacity for personal change and transformation? You as a human being have been travelling the most extraordinary road of change since the day of your conception – and you have managed those changes remarkably well.

Whatever kind of change you are facing now, whether you are reacting to change or have a dream or an ambition that you want to fulfil, to achieve change, especially individual change, you must first identify, or clarify, your Vision.

Buzan's Tools for Transformation

2. Vision and Focus

In Chapter 8 you will meet Change Masters through time who held ambitions and faced challenges akin to the ones facing you in your life. They beat all odds to turn their dreams into reality; they have many qualities in common with each other, and with you. Their primary tool for achieving change was to focus first on their Vision. Your Vision is in constant transition as you explore new concepts and ideas.

■ Vision

Your Vision is your brain's ability to create a distant horizon and on that horizon to create a perfect image of your Utopian ideal. That image needs to be beautifully coloured, magnificently formed, radiant in its energy and congruity, pristine in its clarity, appealing to all your senses and vibrant in its energy.

It needs to be completely seductive in the best and most beautiful interpretation of that word. It needs to draw you towards it inexorably and inevitably with a gravity that is universal in its power. When you create such a Vision, the very vision you have created will take on a life of its own, and as you move towards it, it will increasingly embrace you.

Any mind-calming technique, from music to meditation to daydreaming, will allow your brain to change its state and become more receptive to new influences and adjustment.

▓ Focus

Focus is an extraordinary quality of intelligence that when directed is like a laser. It is precise, goal-directed and phenomenally strong. When you are 'focused' you develop a laser-like energy that is also a gravitational energy that grounds your activity. Focus will determine your action; it will determine the direction (the focus) of all your senses; it will determine the gathering of your thoughts and the direction in which they pay attention. Focus becomes the puppeteer of the actions of your body and its force. It will be driven by your desire to achieve your Vision and your Goals. Its passion will attract other people or things around you. It is an astonishingly powerful mental tool, and it will therefore direct the *course* of your change.

The ability to focus and to *commit* to the vision of that focus is one of the prime tools for bringing about change. In managing change, you need to *focus* on that which you *can* influence. You need to manage the manager of the change, and the manager is you – via your brain and your body.

▓ Forms of change

Change takes many forms: it may be physiological, emotional, material or practical. It also has many rhythms: fast, slow, steady or cataclysmic. It may be perceived as positive or negative depending on whether it has been instigated by us, or inflicted upon us. It may be localized, affecting only ourselves and our families, or may be far-reaching – impacting on the balance of the whole world.

In the sections on Natural, Advised, Anticipated and Enforced Change, I will show you how to transform your attitude to keep your Vision on track.

▓ Embracing natural change

There is one type of change over which we have no control, but of which we are an integral part. I am referring to the natural rhythm of change that continues regardless of the desires and motivation of humankind, through the seasons, via the elements, influencing every aspect of our lives as the world turns on its axis and continues in its orbit in the universe. As the proverb states: 'Time and tide wait for no man' (or woman or child!), and natural change is to be embraced through every stage of life and personal growth from birth to death, from generation to generation. The metaphors throughout this book demonstrate how much we can learn from the natural world of which we are a part – although we so often behave as if we were separate from it.

Tide Laws

The Universal tide
Of Change
Sweeps plankton, slavelike, along

Dolphins ride
The rhythms
Dolphins think
Dolphins decide
Dolphins ride

The tides of Change

To keep your Vision on track, pay attention to the rhythms of your body and where you are in time to assess whether you have chosen the right time in your life to focus on this particular goal. If you are confident that it is a realistic goal, then recognize that you will need to anticipate and go with the natural change, rather than fight against it.

In Chapter 5 you will also be introduced to the concept known as TEFCAS, which provides a bridge between the physical world and the mind to allow us to use the physical laws to interpret change.

Natural change scenario

A couple in their mid-30s enjoy their lifestyle and are moving steadily upwards in their respective careers. He wants children 'at some point'; she is not so sure.

The 'no action' approach

Action: **No action.**

Potential for: Missing the moment. The natural change here is that the woman's fertility will reduce further with each year that passes.

Result: **Change.**

They will become older. The unresolved issue/ lack of focus on the long term may cause problems in the relationship later.

The 'action' approach

Action: **Focus.** Deep discussion.

Potential for: Deeper knowledge and understanding of each other, their relationship and their true desires. Planning for the long term.

Result: **Change.**

They will become older. They are moving towards a joint vision. They will have decided as a couple whether or not to have children. They will be aware of the time frame for their decision. They may decide to opt for assisted reproduction or adoption as a later alternative.

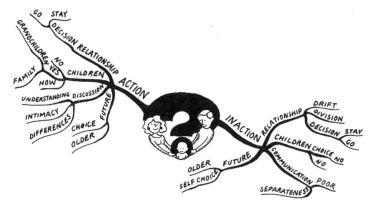

Mind mapping the future as a couple

■ Accepting advised change

There is another category of change that will affect us in different ways, depending upon the circumstances of the change and how far the advice given takes us from where we ideally want to be. Advised change is change that we are recommended to make by a third party, whether a parent, doctor, employer, friend or other advisor who offers advice on how to improve or make changes to health, relationships, language skills, working practices and so on. Whether we feel we have been forced to make the change and choose denial over acceptance or whether we choose to follow the advice and plan for change will depend on a number of factors, but crucially will depend on our personal attitude.

Advised change scenario

A single mother would like to be spending more time with her young daughter. She has thought about starting her own business – but feels trapped by worry about financial commitments. She is tempted to 'just do it' but has been cautioned against hasty action and advised to take professional advice.

The 'no action' approach

Action: **No action.**

Potential for: Increased financial outgoings to pay for third-party care and 'guilt' gifts for her daughter, increased resentment and sadness that she is missing out on motherhood, reduced motivation at work and the possibility of an impulsive decision to change.

Result: **Change.**

Daughter grows up. Either the mother will feel she has missed out on quality time with her daughter or she may leap into change impulsively and endanger the financial future for them both.

The 'action' approach

Action: **Focus.** Research into financial resources, skills stock-take, 'reality' check regarding whether to become self-employed, Discussion with parents and teachers over the pros and cons for her child.

Potential for: Increased self-awareness and confidence-boost, previous delayed decision becomes conscious forward-plan based on financial realities; the confidence that the personal decision to stay put is right for her and her child.

Result: **Change.**

Daughter grows up. Parent–child bond strengthened. Increased professional confidence that comes from making a proactive choice to maintain the status quo in the short term, and to plan for change in the longer term.

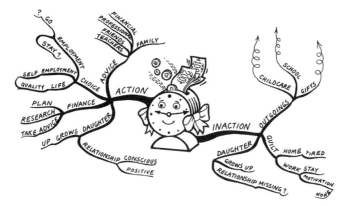

A single mother Mind Maps the alternatives for her future with her daughter

■ Managing anticipated change

Change that we choose for ourselves, or that we have had time to anticipate, is usually experienced as Positive because we are managing it on some level, living it consciously, and therefore feel *stable* within the change. We have had an opportunity to prepare for, drive or influence the outcome of the change.

Planned change may take the form of a developmental milestone or life event, including starting school, puberty, taking exams, first love, first sexual experience, leaving home, starting work, giving birth, getting married, choosing to divorce, changing job, moving house, travelling in retirement. It also encompasses personal development such as choosing to learn a new skill or hobby, starting a new business, enjoying music, continuing education, becoming more healthy, listening more, praising more, trying new ways of living.

On a global or economic level, planned change includes business entrepreneurship, political involvement, volunteering, community involvement, enjoying friends, or travelling.

It is human nature to crave stability as well as excitement. The word stabilize is defined as 'to render steady or stable … to maintain, or regulate the equilibrium of', which raises the interesting paradox that if you manage change well, you do stabilize. That is, you move through the early period of (creative) disruption to a situation of calm and continuous accomplishment.

Anticipated change scenario

A departmental head whose department has been underperforming because of external economic factors beyond her immediate control knows that the status quo cannot be maintained. There are resulting threats to:

- jobs: her own and her staff's;
- profits: the company's and shareholders';
- morale: across the company;
- self-esteem: her own, and those she is responsible for.

The 'no action' approach

Action: **No action.**

Potential result: Personal job loss, staff redundancy.

Result: **Change.**

The ostrich approach. Resistance to change does not prevent change – it means that you will be acted upon instead of acting.

The 'action' approach

Action: **Focus.** Reaction. A change in departmental policy.

Potential result: Personal job loss, staff redundancy, a change in departmental policy.

Result: **Change.**

When change is inevitable, conscious involvement in the forthcoming process means that a transformation is possible, and is likely to mean that you will feel more positive about the result, even if it is negative.

Neither of these scenarios is necessarily comfortable. The chances are, however, that depending on how the process is handled, in the second scenario, the manager's self-esteem is likely to be left intact. They will be able to influence the change process and feel more positive about the outcome.

Result: A potentially negative change can be experienced as something positive.

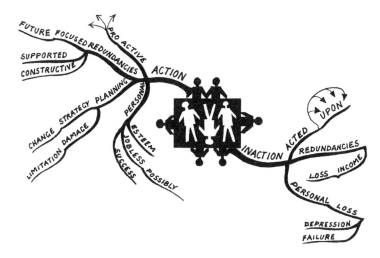

The Mind Map for a departmental head facing major change

■ Stabilizing through change

Stabilization is, quite simply, managing change in a way that maintains the structure and environment of the change but in a desired or productive form.

One way to understand this and to stabilize oneself in the face of thinking about change is to use the metaphor of two giant rivers. It is important that we think of them as giant because of the immense combined energy they would have.

■ Two rivers

Where rivers meet and join, you would think that there would be a synergetic fusing and multiplying of the energies, but what actually happens is complete turmoil. If you place yourself at the junction of two enormous and powerful rivers, you will see two very smooth rivers moving along nicely each in their own direction. At the moment that they meet, however, what was once smooth becomes majestically eruptive. There are unexpected and dizzying waterspouts, tremendous whirlpools, tumultuous waves, eddies venturing backwards as well as forwards – all kinds of chaos and turmoil resulting from the coming together of these energetic forces. However, look a little further downstream and you will see that the two giant energies have synthesized, worked out their joint energies into a single, much greater multiplied ongoing energy. Although the process of change itself is not always smooth, further on down the time stream there is a powerhouse of potential, and the potential for periods of wonderful equanimity. Equanimity often requires disruption in order to establish it on a larger, broader, deeper, more profound and fundamental basis.

It's because two energies are coming together and creating *momentary* turmoil that people often assume that change is negative; but if you are a Change Thinker, you realize that just a little further downstream that mass of energy, the sheer weight and tonnage of it, smoothes out and calms things down.

Hence a river like the Amazon becomes a giant, smooth, miles-plus wide expanse of relatively still water, whereas a little brook remains in constant disruption, its burbling water seriously disrupted by something as small as a pebble. The river of change runs deeper when two powerful energies combine, resulting in a surface of calmness – thus giving rise to the understanding that 'still waters run deep'.

Every relationship, every marriage, every creative business partnership, every community, every period of war and peace experiences this turbulence. In a new relationship, the turbulence takes the form of the excitement of passion and emotional uncertainty; in a marriage periods of calm can disrupt into turmoil if the joint energies are not harnessed and 'looking together in the same direction', to quote Antoine de St-Exupéry. Once you have combined your energies, in a congruent manner, there will tend to be greater depth and calmness in the relationship.

Groups of people fighting for a common cause, a political party organizing itself prior to a general election, a community channelling its energy to gain new resources and services – all these examples of synergistic fusion will follow the same pattern of the two rivers metaphor. The energy of the turbulence is harnessed in order to bring about change; the probability of achieving this is more likely if the group can stabilize itself within the process of change.

If the process of change is not managed well, or the need for the alliance is removed, then disruption accelerates, the river's banks will be flooded, there will be a powerhouse of destruction and untold damage – until the source of the energy stabilizes again.

■ Transforming enforced change

The difference between Planned change and Enforced change is one of personal perception and involvement in that change.

When our familiar world becomes no longer familiar, as a result of unexpected or enforced change, it is natural to retreat initially into a negative response as a way of attempting to regain control. Sometimes we stay there – for too long. 'Familiarity and Risk Avoidance' may appear to equal 'Comfort and Security' initially, but in time may also come to equal 'No Growth and Stagnation'.

In the late nineteenth century, naturalist Charles Darwin saw that in order to survive in the world and avoid extinction, organisms need to adapt to their changing surroundings. As individuals we too might find that if we resist change while things around us are changing, it may be us, rather than 'our world', that becomes 'extinct'.

Enforced change, where you are more acted upon than proactive, is often perceived initially as negative, because it comes as a shock. You have not had time to adjust to the process of change; in response you may feel yourself to be a victim of circumstance. This type of change can lead to short-term feelings of loss of control. This is especially true if the change is cataclysmic, bringing about sudden, transformative change.

Examples of forced change may include chronic illness, life-changing injury, emotional abandonment, unexpected job loss, unplanned pregnancy, unforeseen financial or material loss, personal betrayal or the sudden death of a loved one. On global and economic levels, forced change could include recession, war, terrorist attacks, reduced health-care provision, increases in taxation, inefficient transport networks, and so on.

Painful as the situation may be, enforced change must be handled in the same way as all other change situations. Cataclysmic changes *are* going to happen to each of us at some point in our lives. They *are* inevitable. They may be extremely painful. We have no option or choice in these matters.

The choice you *do* have, as always, is whether to become a victim of the situation and your emotions, or whether to ride it like the Surf Rider (see page 24), learning from it, managing it and helping others to manage it too, in the most positive way possible.

■ Transforming events

You may ask, how can you possibly change catastrophically negative events into positive ones? The truth is that even if there is no doubting the physical outcome of the situation, you still have choice and influence. Once the initial shock has subsided and you have had time to assess the impact of the event, it is entirely possible to see the situation differently, and to choose a response that transforms the forced change into something positive.

If you find yourself resisting change, the associated emotions may also relate to a sense of loss of *self*. If for example you resist change by staying in an unhealthy relationship because it is comfortable and you are afraid of being on your own; if you continue your workaholic patterns even though they are killing you by inches because you are scared of the vacuum in the world outside of work; if you won't stop drinking or smoking even though you have been diagnosed with the early signs of heart disease because you believe it will be a farewell to your youth and your lifestyle; then you need to

pause

and take the time to reassess your vision of the future in relation to your immediate goals. Where are you now? Acted upon or proactive? Do your present actions tally with your desired expectations for five or ten years' time?

Remember – resisting change does not prevent change from happening, it simply means the change will happen in a way that takes you further from where you ideally want to be.

■ Phases of change

Five phases are commonly associated with recovering from radical change. These are:

Denial ➤ Anger ➤ Bargaining ➤ Depression ➤ Acceptance

Your immediate response to dramatic change may be denial, numbness, fear, shock, anger or tears. You may find yourself in turmoil – until you find a way to change gear, take action and regain personal control and flow within the rhythm of the situation. At these times of difficulty you may find refuge in laughter. Laughter is, as the adage goes, 'the best medicine'.

The time to realize that you are still in turbulence – resisting, rather than merging with the event or situation – is when your feelings are running out of control, or your body is showing signs of nervous tension. You may feel confused, emotionally empty or constantly exhausted. The following symptoms are signs that it is time to seek support and help from others.

■ You have to keep active in order to avoid experiencing your feelings.
■ You find yourself bursting into tears at the slightest provocation.
■ You have no-one with whom to share your emotions.
■ Your relationships are suffering, or sexual problems develop.
■ You are smoking, drinking or taking drugs to excess.
■ You keep having accidents.
■ Your performance at work is suffering.
■ Those around you are becoming vulnerable to your moods.
■ You suffer continuously from nightmares and sleep poorly.
■ You are suffering from exhaustion.
■ You feel totally alone.

If these symptoms apply to you, it is important to recognize that you may choose to make medical services and counsellors part of your personal support network for a while (see Chapter 8 on how to choose and use the support of Change Masters).

Enforced change scenario

A man discovers his partner has been having an affair. To confront the situation is to make it 'real' and therefore to risk losing the stability of the status quo. To ignore it is to increase potential for unhappiness and suspicion – but the illusion is that it will maintain the status quo.

The 'no action' approach

Action: **No action.**

Potential result: Suppression of feelings. Negative feelings towards partner, loss of self-esteem, gradual and painful erosion of relationship.

Result: **Change.** Possible loss. Long-term pain.

The 'action' approach

Action: **Focus.** Reaction.

               Discussion, acknowledgment of feelings, shared response.

Potential result: Changed feelings towards partner, discussion with partner, joint action plan – which could lead either to staying together or agreeing to part.

Result: **Change.** Possible loss. Possible gain. Transformative.

Both these processes are painful and will involve change 'for better or worse', but in the second scenario there is conscious involvement and a sense of personal choice – not chance.

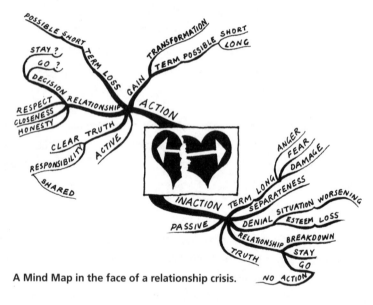

A Mind Map in the face of a relationship crisis.

In order to recover from the distress of radical or cataclysmic change, it is crucial to be consciously aware of what is happening to you and how you are feeling. The techniques outlined in *Embracing Change* will enable you to re-focus your future, adjust your ultimate goal, to know that even at your lowest (or highest) ebb, you are not a victim of fate, but a Change Maker in charge of your own destiny.

Paradox

Remain
Constant
By Changing

Stay where you are
By Moving

All this is a dream. Still, examine it by a few experiments. Nothing is too wonderful to be true, if it be consistent with the laws of nature.

Michael Faraday, *Notebook*

Chapter 5
How you change

❏ Buzan's Tools for Transformation: 3. TEFCAS

During the course of your life, change will occur no matter what you do to anticipate it, no matter how you plan and no matter how you resist it. It will occur in ways you can never have anticipated and will be more wonderful, more challenging, more joyful, more unpredictable, more enlightening, more enriching, more rewarding and on occasion more heart-breaking than you can have ever imagined.

Every time you decide to take an action, there is a subsequent effect that you will learn from. This powerful and natural process is called TEFCAS and it is our next Tool for Transformation.

Buzan's Tools for Transformation

3. TEFCAS

TEFCAS is an acronym for the stages of learning and self-review that the body and mind can't help but follow. It is a process that is happening all the time. Each is vitally important; each one leads to the next. When you are in the process of change, following these steps consciously will transform your ability to change in the way you desire. Once you have understood the concept you will see very clearly where you are in the process of change and improvement in any situation.

TEFCAS can be described as the scientific method applied to your life. Each of the six letters stands for one of six 'laws' describing the way in which the brain has *no choice* but to work. TEFCAS is an established physical process, a universal fact.

TEFCAS stands for:

- Try
- Event
- Feedback
- Check
- Adjust
- Success

But how does it work? How can you apply TEFCAS to the complex changes you are facing in your life today and in the future? The first part of that answer is that, although change is complex, all change can be broken into more simple parts. This is included in the process of identifying your

Vision and applying *Focus* (see Chapter 4). Once you have truly identified what it is you are trying to achieve, you can begin to do just that – by Trying.

Many people never Try to achieve their ambitions because they look at where they are starting in relation to their goal, and they focus on the gap in between – which appears absolutely gigantic. They may think: What's the point?, seeing only that it will take massive effort with no certainty of success. Lifting a 300lb weight may seem impossible when you weigh only 100lb, and you are bound to think 'I'll never do that'; but few weight lifters are able to lift 300lb when they first begin training. Bit by bit, day by day, workout-by-workout in the gym, strength is slowly built up until they bring about the change that they want, both in their body and the weight they are able to lift.

■ A leap of faith

Fiona is an enthusiastic and inventive teacher with a passion for mathematics. She was assigned to an unruly class of ten-year-olds who had lost complete confidence in their ability to do maths. In order to gain their attention and to take the first step towards making maths an approachable subject, she posed a question.

Standing by the door and looking nine metres across the room to the window, she asked them: 'Who believes I could *jump* from one side of this classroom to the other?' There was stunned silence and looks of utter disbelief. Did this new teacher think they were totally stupid? There was a chorus of uncertain 'no'. Eventually one child said, 'Of course you can't, unless you are the world long-jump champion.'

Fiona held her ground. 'Aha – but I can,' she declared, 'and what's more, I believe that *you* can too.' Again there were looks of utter disbelief, but by now she had their complete attention. Fiona began to jump: half a metre, followed by another half metre and another and another and so on, until she reached the window. She turned to the class: 'You see – *any of you* could jump across this room. Maths is like that too. We will take one jump at a time – until we have all made it across the room, all the way from the door to the window. Are you with me?' There was a chorus of 'yes' and a roomful of smiles. With that first jump, they had each taken their first step, their first TRY towards certain success.

■ How TEFCAS works

To illustrate how TEFCAS works, I am going to assume that as part of your Change Programme you have decided to take up Juggling. Juggling offers the multiple benefits of improving your hand–eye coordination, changing your physical health for the better, as well as reducing your levels of tension. It will also have the benefit of enabling me to demonstrate TEFCAS in clear fashion.

■ Step One: Try

To bring about change (improvement) in your behaviours you must first make the *effort* and the *choice* to TRY to change. This means, both physically and mentally, taking *practical* and *active* steps towards achieving your aim.

Inherent within trying is the taking of a *risk*. In the case of learning to juggle, the TRYING means first making the effort to choose to *throw the ball*. This means running the risk that you may not achieve your aim – of catching it.

Change Makers learn to be good risk takers, who understand that when you try something, there *is* the possibility of *not* accomplishing your goal (in the old-fashioned vocabulary of the twentieth century, 'failing' – see page 83). A Change Maker also knows *with certainty* that *without* trying there is absolutely *no* possibility of achieving any goal. In the early stages of learning, the odds of *not* achieving your ultimate goal immediately are high. A Change Maker takes this in his stride, recognizes that there is a process of learning ahead and indeed welcomes the *frisson* (thrill) of the experiment, of having a hypothesis or idea of what is going to happen.

Equally, the Change Maker knows that when you Try there is the possibility of *accomplishing* your goal (Success); If they are wise they will also know that things will usually turn out slightly differently from the original Utopian vision …

Every time you TRY, you reduce by One
the number of Tries left before you reach your goal.

When you TRY there will follow, by definition, an EVENT.

■ Step Two: Event

Once you have Tried, the subsequent EVENT is inevitable. It is at this single stage of the Change process that the universe, and not you, has total control.

When your juggler-self has thrown the ball, the laws of physics dictate that there *will be* an Event: the ball will *land*. It *may* land in your hand (hurrah!), or it may land on the ground, on your head, in your partner's coffee cup. The universe does not care *where* it lands, but land it will.

Your response to this event is your choice. You may choose to respond negatively: 'I can't', 'I will never', 'I won't', 'I'm a failure'. You may choose to respond positively: 'I am in the process of learning', 'I am amused', 'I will improve next time'.

Every EVENT in life can take you closer to achieving your goal.

Your choice of response, i.e. your Attitude, will dictate at this point whether you choose to gain benefit from the next stage in the TEFCAS process, because the universe does not leave you unsupported. Following every Event, the universe, in the guise of facts, friends, your responses, the responses of others, will provide you with the gift of FEEDBACK, which will take you one step closer to reaching your goal.

■ Step Three: Feedback

After every Event the universe will shower you with billions of tiny gifts. These gifts come in the form of FEEDBACK and they are being given to you every second of your life. For every Event provides you with information through your senses. Your senses are the most sophisticated instruments in the known universe, making even the most complex of the world's mechanical, visual and auditory machines look ridiculously simple and inefficient by comparison.

You can choose whether or not to look at, or listen to, or feel or smell or taste the Feedback; it may not always be comfortable – but if you choose to pay attention to it you will move ever closer towards your goal.

How do you experience Feedback as a novice juggler? You will receive an extraordinary amount as a result of throwing the ball and watching it land. Your eye will receive trillions of pieces of information about where the ball went: its trajectory, speed and energy. Your ears will hear the ball 'whistle' through the air and will hear the thud of its landing. Your spatial self will give you information about the rhythm in which you threw the balls, and an estimation of how high you threw them. Your sense of touch will give you subtle information about texture and weight and resilience, and also the degree of tension there was in your hands as you prepared to throw and release the balls. Your body will feed back to you millions of types of muscular information about the degree of energy directed towards the throwing of the ball.

Thus it is at the Feedback stage that you have the most help and choice to bring about change. The prime choice is to choose to receive and consider as much of the feedback as you can. To be a good learner you need to be in tune with all your senses, to use all your powers of observation and intuition.

Receive Feedback with an open mind and encourage it from those whom you know and trust. This Feedback will be of high quality and particularly valuable. The art of managing change and becoming an *effective* Change Manager includes learning to deal appropriately with the trillions of gifts you are consistently receiving.

**Every time you choose to pay attention to FEEDBACK
you will move closer to succeeding in your goal.**

A master of change is also a master of learning and will endeavour to use the brain and the potential of the brain to its optimum capacity and in the way in which it was designed.

Leonardo da Vinci stated that his main goal in life was to develop his senses. This he did, and in so doing was able to receive from the universe almost infinitely more information (Feedback!) than other people. You can do the same as Leonardo did.

Before acting upon the Feedback it is important to CHECK the feedback, to ensure that the information given is fully understood in an appropriate way.

■ Step Four: Check

When your brain has gathered all the information generously provided for you by the universe, it will CHECK that Feedback on both a conscious and unconscious level.

It is at this stage that you have the freedom to decide the extent to which you take on board the feedback – from yourself, from friends, from family and from others. You have the option of glossing over or ignoring the feedback, or of analysing it with as much clarity, precision, logic and creativity as you can.

The more honest and constructive you can be with yourself at this stage, the more likely you are to achieve your goal. It is important to note the word 'constructive'. We will explore later how the language of Self-Talk can influence your thinking, your attitude and your likelihood of success. This is not an opportunity to berate yourself, but the stage at which you need to encourage yourself positively to continue with your quest for success.

Having analysed and compared your actual (juggling) performance with previous performances, and with the held ideal (your eventual goal) in mind, your brain will go into super-logical, super-mathematical mode and will arrive at its next inevitable step.

Every time you CHECK the results of your actions with honesty you will focus more clearly on what you need to do to reach your goal.

Just as your brain has no choice but to change – so it will have no choice but to ADJUST its response on the basis of the feedback.

■ Step Five: Adjust

How will you ADJUST? Adjustment is a stage of major personal freedom and is closely linked to your levels of desire and motivation. The level of your desire for change and the ways in which you Adjust will significantly affect the probability of your ultimate Success. To help you Adjust with more skill and effectiveness, you may wish to review your previous trials, and the input from your network of personal Change Masters (see Chapter 8), books, professional advisors, libraries, friends, magazines, clubs, videos, audios, and any other sources of information relevant to the change you are bringing about.

1 If your desire to succeed at juggling is low, you might decide at this stage that your lack of progress is frustrating and quit juggling immediately!

2. If your desire to succeed is high, you might decide to Adjust your throw, your posture, the lighting, your position, or the weight of the juggling balls in order to increase your opportunity to succeed.

3. If in refocusing you decide that learning to juggle is no longer an appropriate goal because, for example, your need to take up a team sport is of greater priority, you might Adjust your goal and decide to learn to play football instead.

Beware of the third option. Before deciding to change direction ensure that you have Checked the previous Feedback with honesty. Is the declared motive really the deciding factor, or is there something that you are not acknowledging?

One thing is certain – you *will* have to Adjust. There is no way out of it. Even if you decide you are not going to Adjust, you will still have adjusted, by adjusting your behaviour towards greater rigidity and lack of change. Therefore, you *have* changed!

**Every time you Adjust your actions
and increase your desire to succeed,
you simultaneously increase the probability
of reaching your goal.**

What have these five steps been leading up to? To your inevitable SUCCESS in accomplishing your goal; or your next step on your journey towards achieving a more desired form of change.

■ Step Six: Success

Your sixth and final stage *is* therefore SUCCESS. We are talking here about Success on many levels. When you first begin to juggle, you may measure Success as catching a single ball; as you progress through various stages of learning towards your ultimate goal of juggling eight balls, your targets will increase. If you are learning appropriately, are paying attention to the TEFCAS process, you will improve gradually and steadily, moving ever closer to achieving your ultimate goal. TEFCAS will continue in a cyclical spiral, moving ever upwards through many successes, towards your ultimate Success.

If you are trying to learn inappropriately, and are not listening to the Feedback, or are not Checking and Adjusting accordingly, you may not move beyond Trying and the subsequent Event. It will therefore take you much longer to achieve your goal, and you may never get there.

Remember TEFCAS is not a straight line with a start and end point, it is a continuous spiral: *TEFCAS*

■ Learning through TEFCAS

Changes that take place from babyhood through childhood are absolutely astonishing and as adults we can learn a lot from observing attitude, motivation and determination during those early stages. Babies, especially, love change and are the ultimate negotiators of it.

Every parent knows that when a child is learning to speak or to walk, there is rarely an immediate leap from single word to whole sentences, or from first steps to confident walking. Instead there is a gradual process of assimilation and confidence-building. Children are TEFCAS in motion, always ready to learn from the Feedback surrounding them and to tackle the next Trial in intrepid fashion.

First steps (**Try**) usually lead to first fall (**Event**). Tears and fears then trigger a hasty retreat back to the safety of the crawling phase (**Feedback**) and a learning 'plateau' (**Check**) until the child is 'ready' to put conceptual skills (**Adjust**) into practical use (**Success**). The gaps between thought and deed become shorter as experience and confidence grow. Likewise, a toddler who has learnt a few words will retreat into 'baby talk' when tired or attention seeking. Sometimes, moving 'forwards' can be too much. A fallow period of 'sleep' and assimilation is much more valuable than pushing against natural limits, and it is in these quiet times that integration and learning is consolidated.

If the period of discomfort were not eventually overcome, we would never learn to walk. Amazingly, we *do* learn to walk. We try, try and TRYYYY again – and our experience of the world expands accordingly. We have an infinite capacity for change – once we are ready to embrace it.

This process continues throughout life. We are infinitely complex beings. Even as adults, we learn in stages – our learning curves follow the TEFCAS process, proceeding upwards and downwards, in peaks and troughs. Adults, too, 'plateau' or appear to go backwards as we take time to assimilate our new-found knowledge and understanding of ourselves (and the world) before gathering momentum and becoming ready to proceed forwards again to begin the next stage.

■ Feeding the vision

When Elizabeth was in her early 40s she decided to take steps to realize a long-held ambition. She left her career in nursing to focus on setting up her own gardening business. She had 'green fingers' and a passion for garden design, but was not naturally commercial. She invested in becoming fully trained as a qualified designer, and now, with one year of her degree course left to go, was focused on finding clients. She felt she had done all the right things – distributed a marketing brochure, made proactive phone calls, followed up business leads, but still had no clients. She rang a close friend in a moment of despair.

'Everything I do is going nowhere. It's not that I haven't been Trying – I have. Net result – nothing! I feel as if I'm wasting my time. All I have after weeks of Trying is fewer resources, lower motivation and a growing feeling of despair. I can feel myself panicking. What will I do if all my training has been wasted? I can feel my thoughts going in a negative, downward spiral. What's more, my back has given out – so I can't work now anyway.'

Elizabeth was unfamiliar with the concept of TEFCAS at the time and so had misunderstood where she was in the TEFCAS process. Because of the level of effort she was putting in and the personal discomfort she was experiencing, she assumed she should be nearing Success; in fact, she was still at the Feedback stage, gaining knowledge she hadn't realized she needed.

Elizabeth's situation shows that Trying does not always lead to an immediately visible and fast Event. Her Feedback was saying, 'You have to *Keep On Trying* in order to achieve the event you require.'

Elizabeth Checked her Feedback by talking to her friend. The friend pointed out that she had not had a negative result, she just hadn't had the result she needed – yet. She needed to Adjust her perspective. The valuable lesson she was learning at this key stage in her new business development was the reality of the length of time it takes to secure new clients.

Elizabeth Adjusted her approach as a result; she not only re-contacted previous leads, she regained the impetus to follow up new ones. The result: by the end of the week she had moved closer towards gaining commitment from three potential new clients. By the end of the fortnight she had contracts with two of the three. Result: hard-earned, *realistic*, steady growth. Real Success – and renewed positive energy.

TEFCAS taught Elizabeth to understand the commercial realities of her new business, to learn to Keep on Trying – past her personal comfort zone – in order to acquire new customers as part of the *ongoing* process of business development.

Elizabeth's experience also shows the value of personal mentors and Change Masters. In times of despair we all need to revisit our Vision of reality by feeding it from the OUTSIDE.

Action point

Take a moment to consider your current Goal or Vision. Where are you in the TEFCAS process? Are you feeling disheartened through non-result? If so, have you Checked your Feedback? Have you asked your friends or other advisors for their honest view? Do you need to Adjust your approach and Try again?

■ Success as a goal in itself

Each interim success en route to your ultimate goal can give you a euphoric sense of achievement. Enjoy and appreciate the moment; you deserve it. This is the feeling that will spur you on to ever-greater things as you review and refine your ultimate vision in your quest for ongoing positive change.

A word of caution is needed, however. There can be a serious pitfall in achieving success if you do not recognize that it *is* a mere moment in an ongoing process of change. The danger is that in deciding to bring about, and then achieving, a positive change, you become so happy with the success that you stop Trying, and are tempted to remain static, basking in your own brilliance. Then, of course, you are likely to become complacent and revert to a state of relatively less activity.

We know that, according to the laws of physics, it takes a lot more energy to move something from a state of inertia than it does to maintain the momentum of something that is already in motion. Beware therefore that you *Do Not*, in your moment of triumph, *Stop* – thereby reducing the probability that you will bring about change in the future.

■ Beware the negative goal

Achieving your goal may sound as if it should always be a positive thing, and as TEFCAS is an inevitable process, you could be duped into believing that everything you achieve is good. However, beware. Your success could also be a dangerous swamp into which you could unknowingly be lured. How?

If your desired change is one that is fundamentally *damaging or injurious* to you, then your success in bringing about that (negative) change will lead you on a non-virtuous spiral – into the pits! Such inappropriate goals could include choosing to remain in an abusive relationship, successfully undertaking a criminal act, causing malicious harm to another person or reverting to a meta-negative habit.

Your success goal must therefore be a positive-to-positive goal in which the success you are going to bring about will manifest in a change that will be of advantage to you; *not* one that can entrap you downwards on the slippery slope of the negative spiral.

■ Choice within TEFCAS

If TEFCAS is inevitable, then where is your choice within this inevitable sequence of events?

Answer: Everywhere!

Consider the way that gravity keeps you on the surface of the earth, by pulling your body towards the earth's core. Does this mean that you are held as an inactive blob of protoplasm, stuck to one point of the planet's surface? No! The force of gravity provides you with freedom. Instead of floating off from the planet's surface into space like a giant piece of flotsam, you have the choice to move, run, dance, walk, do athletics, play, climb trees and mountains, swim rivers and oceans. You are anchored by gravity – but have fundamentally *limitless* freedom. The same is true of TEFCAS – which of course is implicit within the laws of gravity also.

As a Change Thinker you have the choice of whether or not to Try in the first place, and how frequently to continue to Try. A good Change Thinker will Try far more than the average person. A pantheon of great geniuses is peopled by individuals who Tried many more times and at many more things than those who did not become great. It was this very willingness to *keep* Trying that eventually led to their discoveries. This is evidenced by the famous tale of Thomas Edison, who reportedly Tried over 6,000 experiments before discovering the light bulb.

The process of TEFCAS envelops you in a process of truth and change that gives you security, while highlighting the inevitability of change. Within that absolute you have phenomenal freedom of choice. If you learn the art and science of playing with TEFCAS to your advantage, the changes you bring about will always be the ones you desire.

It is invaluable to realize here that *the universe and your brain conspire to guide and direct you towards succeeding in everything you do*. In preparing for change in your life, it is very comforting to know that your brain is *obliged* to deal with change. As a Change Thinker, you are also an agent for Success in the continuing process of change.

TEFCAS is a tool for dealing with change in every aspect of daily life.

▓ Reinterpreting 'failure'

A word about 'failure' is needed at this point because most people are very disheartened, or may become aggressively demotivated, if they don't achieve the results they were envisioning very soon after embarking on their chosen path. 'Failure' is quite simply the result of misanalysis of an Event or of the

Feedback. The Event is not the same as the Ultimate Goal; it is an essential step on the pathway to achieving that Goal. Failure is in fact a form of Success, in that every time you Try, you risk failure, as you can never learn without the risk of making a mistake. Every resulting Event gives you Feedback, and therefore every Event is an information node on the path to bringing about better-informed change.

TEFCAS encourages you to accept the result of the Event for what it is, and to accept your gifts of Feedback from the nurturing universe; then to get on with bringing about change, positive change, as fast as you possibly can.

■ TEFCAS in action

Named after the ship that took Charles Darwin on his world tour of exploration and discovery, the 2004 Beagle 2 mission is a superb example of TEFCAS in action. Generally reported as 'unsuccessful' by the press, Professor Colin Pillinger's quest to land *Beagle* on Mars was in fact an immense accomplishment that has provided untold benefits and Feedback for future Mars missions.

Everything about Professor Pillinger: his brilliance, his enthusiasm, determination and entrepreneurial spirit, mark him out as a revolutionary Change Thinker and Change Maker. He has been disarmingly frank about his early scientific achievements. 'Every time I mixed two solutions together, the results blew up and ended up all over the ceiling,' he told Robin McKie of the *Observer* in 2002. Clearly he kept **T**rying and as a result of subsequent **E**vents took this early **F**eedback on board, **C**hecked and **A**djusted his techniques and progressed **S**uccessfully to become Professor of Planetary Science at the Open University in the UK. In Beagle 2, he created the first British-built object to reach another world.

From the outset the Beagle 2 project overcame obstacle after obstacle after obstacle. Pillinger paid total attention to detail, he was flexible, astonishingly creative and directed the project to a phenomenal success. He had to raise much of the early funding for the project himself, with other financial support coming from popular musicians and the art world.

The mission aimed to get a spacecraft into exact orbit around Mars in order to monitor and photograph the planet's surface. In conjunction, a tiny landing craft was added at the last moment – the little *Beagle* itself – which was both a satellite and a sub-spaceship. At the time the craft disappeared on Christmas Day 2003, the Beagle 2 project was already 90 per cent successful.

Every single reaction of Colin Pillinger to every single challenge was creatively directed towards finding and solving, and if not finding then immediately moving on to the next stage of exploration. He achieved 100 per cent success in getting the mission approved in 'insurmountable' circumstances, he achieved 100 per cent success in having the craft ejected perfectly, he achieved 100 per cent success in successfully orbiting Mars while operating perfectly. He then directed the landing craft towards the surface of Mars – perfectly, and it then disappeared, perhaps falling into a crater that no-one could have predicted. Unjustly termed 'failure' by the press and some other authorities, this is clearly an astonishing success by any other measure.

Despite the increasing probability that *Beagle 2* would not be found, Pillinger still held out hope, and he complimented and encouraged and tried to help the Americans in their endeavours with an associated mission to land *Spirit*. He continued to point out that 90 per cent of the mission was extremely successful, not least because the satellite that carried *Beagle* would revolve in orbit around Mars for the following two years while returning ground-breaking pictures to Earth. It would attempt to confirm unequivocally the presence of water on Mars and therefore the probability that there was, at one time, life.

By 26 January 2004, Pillinger was ready to Try again. He commented: 'We will move on to the next phase in the search … We are dedicated to trying to refly Beagle 2 in some shape or form.' He also pointed out that the Beagle project had access to only £45 million, one tenth of the US budget, and yet they succeeded in launching the spacecraft and achieved significant success. He used all the powers of Feedback to demonstrate that *Beagle 2 did* reach Mars's orbit, it *did* disengage from the satellite, it *did* land, and may yet be found and retrieved. Pillinger continued: 'We need to know how far it [*Beagle 2*] got because we need to know which parts of this mission we don't have to study in further detail …' He needed to know the results of the subsequent Event in order to gain true Feedback and to Check that Feedback to Adjust for future Success. His approach was pure TEFCAS-In-Action. His work was cooperative and laid the foundation for further exploration that will span generations. He succeeded in changing the history of the human race and space exploration, and he did it in a *perfectly* Meta-Positive way (see Chapter 7).

PART TWO

Embracing change

Your vision will become clear only when you can look into your own heart. Who looks outside, dreams; who looks inside, awakes.

Carl Gustav Jung

Chapter 6
Self-perception: how to change your world

❏ Buzan's Tools for Transformation: 4. Mind Maps®

❏ The power of transformational processes

❏ What a Mind Map® is

❏ How to read and apply what a Mind Map® reveals

This chapter will introduce you to one of the most powerful tools for learning and personal discovery that you will ever encounter. This technique combines transformational processes that will help you to choose to change, to manage the change process, and to *embrace* changes as they happen, with the understanding that change is the very essence of life and that you can choose to live the life you want to live.

How do we combine these processes? By learning how to use an extraordinary and dynamic tool for change called Mind Maps®. Mind Maps are the key to unlocking the true potential of your amazing mind and to becoming whatever you want to be.

■ What are Mind Maps?®

A Mind Map is drawn in the shape and style of a brain cell and was designed as a tool to encourage the brain to work to optimum efficiency in the style that it does naturally.

In a previous publication, *The Mind Map Book*, I explored the concept of Natural Architecture, using photographic images of trees, plants, leaves and cells from the natural world. These extraordinary structures are amazing and entrancing. We see them every time we look at the veins of a leaf, or the branches of a tree; they are nature's Mind Maps, echoing the shapes of brain cells and reflecting the way we ourselves are created and connected – a clear reminder that the natural world is forever changing, and has an extraordinary capacity for regeneration. We witness this daily through the earth's rotation and the rhythm of the seasons.

An effective Mind Map illustrates the multi-dimensional, often complex process of change in clear, dynamic form. A successful Mind Map is both an image (your Vision) and a visualization, containing within it additional images, which, driven by the constructive power of your imagination, will multiply the power of the picture well beyond the 1,000 words of the old adage 'a picture is worth a thousand words'. Combine the engine of your imagination with a positive attitude and you begin to fire up the process of Change.

Those of you who are familiar with my books will know that I first developed the concept of Mind Mapping as a learning and memory tool while struggling to take effective notes in my student days. My extraordinary experience and immediate personal success led me to realize that Mind Maps could be developed as a powerful tool for personal transformation and a way of realizing our natural abilities. I had a Vision and an ambition that Mind Maps would become a catalyst that would influence a generation of individuals, business thinkers and educators. Thirty years on, with the support and enthusiasm of a growing network of world-class Change Thinkers, it is an immense source of joy and satisfaction to me that people around the world in all walks of life and at all levels now use Mind Maps as a way of optimizing their potential and bringing about personal change.

Mind Mapping for Change reveals us to ourselves and enables us to embrace change with confidence, in the knowledge that we are able to influence our future even when we feel we are more acted upon than acting.

Mind Maps work because the concept already feels familiar. The process mirrors the way we think and succeeds in showing us to ourselves.

A Mind Map will allow you to tap into your true creative self and see clearly:

Where you are	Your problems, your dreams, your ambitions and your ideals.
Who you are	Your unique abilities – at home, in your work, at leisure and in relationships.
How you see yourself	Revealing your true self, and your vision of the future.
How you see the world	Your relationship with others and how you think they see you.
What you want	For yourself, for others, for today, for the future
AND	
How to get there!	

A Mind Map will enable you to Review your Vision, Commit to Change and Make It Real.

To understand why Mind Maps are so effective, first you need to understand more about the way the brain thinks and remembers.

■ The wonder of Radiant Thinking®

Radiant Thinking reflects the way in which your brain works. It is a fundamental expression of the brain's internal processes, focusing on the fact that the brain thinks from central points in images or key words.

The brain does not think in linear, sentential, monochromatic, monotonic ways – all of which forward it into rigid behaviours that decrease the probability of change. The brain thinks in multiple, radiant ways. Radiant Thoughts radiate outwards like the branches of a star or tree, or the rivers flowing from the peak of a snow-capped mountain, or the blood vessels of the body that emanate from the heart.

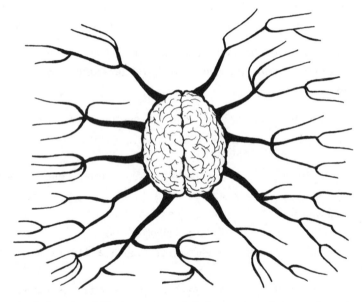

Your brain has the ability to create an infinite number of stars, solar systems, galaxies, and indeed universes of thought inside your head *if* you use it in the correct way. The Mind Map is simply the external manifestation, on the page, of the ways in which your brain thinks. It is the mirror that reflects outside what is inside.

If you wish to become a Change Thinker, you need to begin to think *consciously* in a way that will feed the brain congruently, i.e., by mirroring the way it functions naturally.

Radiant Thinking® exercise

I am now going to demonstrate to you the power of your mind. I am going to ask you to access a piece of information and to check what happens when you call it up.

The piece of information I would like you to access is:

NELSON MANDELA

You did not hear me say the words; nevertheless, now let's check:

WHAT did you get?

How QUICKLY did you get it?

Did you see an IMAGE?

Was there COLOUR in it?

WHERE had it been before it appeared?

It is probable that you will have immediately in your mind's eye the IMAGE of the charismatic former President of South Africa. You may also see COLOUR, or hear MUSIC associated with that period of politics. The image will have appeared instantaneously. You are unlikely to have been left with only the written word in your mind, nor did you need to hear the words to be able to interpret them.

This demonstrates that we all (every male, every female, of every nationality, every language, every racial group) think in images that radiate out in associations. This is the basis of this exercise; it is the basis for all our thinking and is the basis of Mind Maps.

Your brain has the power and the ability to retrieve images from its trillion-fold database instantaneously. It has the ability to make associations between images and to relate them to other factors instantaneously; thereby adapting its thinking to any change situation with an incredible mathematical capacity greater than any known computer. This also demonstrates that you have the ability to change the images and associations that are at the forefront of your thinking instantaneously.

Mind Maps have been devised to enhance and multiply this thought process. They use Radiant Thinking as a primary tool to revolutionize the speed and flexibility of your thought processes in order that you can choose to change – instantaneously!

■ Imagination and Association

The primary language of the brain is not the spoken word, nor the written word; the brain operates by creating associations, via your multiple senses, between a multi-faceted network of *images*, colours, key words and ideas, thereby making connections between the jewels that are your thoughts. No matter what your 'prime' or native language is, that written and spoken language, whether it is English, Spanish, Japanese, Portuguese, Aboriginal Australian or Chinese, is but a *sub-routine* of your thinking.

Mind Maps are a manifestation of the brain's imaging and associative capacity. Two pillars of memory are Imagination and Association and therefore Mind Maps are a multi-dimensional mnemonic technique (for improving memory). They use networks of images and associations to capture the thoughts and feelings of the present, thereby enabling us to keep them as memories for future reference.

A Mind Map therefore is the manifestation of that which allows the brain to speak to itself in its own language. In the words of Dr Ronald Tan, CEO of Singapore Institute of Management:

'The Mind Map is the first truly global language.'

■ Using Mind Maps® as a tool for change

Mind Maps enhance the way you think by enabling your brain to work in a natural and synergistic way. Mind Mapping will encourage your brain to associate, link, connect your thoughts, fears, dreams and ideals in a limitless fashion, enabling you to arrive at ideas, conclusions and plans that you would never otherwise reach.

■ Mind Maps will encourage you to focus on your Vision.

■ Mind Maps are the Change Tool that will bring about the Success that you aimed for when using TEFCAS.

■ Mind Maps encourage you to Try; they are the tool for observing the Event, for gathering and organizing Feedback: they are the tool that helps you then Check that Feedback and they are the tool that helps you Adjust to the Feedback and to establish the Success that your original Mind Map said you were going to have.

■ Mind Maps will enable you to see 'at a glance' whether your Attitude is helping or hindering your progress through change.

■ Mind Maps are the result of a process that will help you to see where you need further help and guidance in order to manage your period of change – and to achieve your aims.

Once you have grasped how to use this simple but powerful concept effectively, your capacity to think creatively will increase immeasurably; your ability to plan, manage and achieve your goals will be unstoppable. Success will be yours for the planning – and the taking.

Buzan's Tools for Transformation
4. Mind Maps®

Before embarking on any form of Mind Map it is essential that you clarify your Vision or Goal. (See Chapter 4.) To clarify your Vision is to make sure that your mental telescope is focused and that each level of magnification is equally clear. The centre of your Mind Map should summarize your Vision, ideally in image form.

It is often useful, in terms of clarifying your Goal, to think about what you would like history to report that you were, or that you accomplished. This has the beneficial effect of focusing you on the very, very long and strategic term and will sharpen dramatically your immediate actions.

The Mind Map that results from this intense Focus will allow your general, strategic Vision to be sharpened, and sharpened further, as you get into the more analytic details.

If you feel torn between more than one Vision, for example between the Vision of a *problem* that you want to resolve: such as resolving your financial crisis; and the Vision of a *dream* that you want to make a reality: such as relocating to the south of France or starting a business, then do two Mind Maps and then review the overlap.

It is *always* possible, although not necessarily immediately, to turn a negative scenario into potential for positive change.

■ Getting started

In order to create effective Mind Maps you will need a stock of paper, multi-coloured pens, at least 10–20 minutes of uninterrupted time – and your brain!

Ensure you have an exercise book or a quantity of good quality LARGE size sheets of BLANK, unlined paper.

Why?

■ You need PLENTY of paper, because you are embarking on a journey. This is not a one-off exercise; you will want to refer back to your Mind Maps over time to review your progress and to review your goals.

■ You need LARGE sized sheets of paper – because you will want space to explore your ideas. Small pages will cramp your style.

■ The pages should be BLANK and UNLINED in order to free the brain to think in an uninhibited and creative way.

■ An exercise book or ring binder of paper is a must because your first Mind Map is the start of a working journal. You don't want to be sub-consciously inhibited because this is a 'special' book for neat writing only, and you will want to keep all your ideas together in order to see how your plans and needs evolve over time.

Purchase an array of multi-COLOURED pens in fine, medium and highlighter thickness that flow easily and with which you can write comfortably and quickly.

Why?

■ Colour stimulates the brain and will activate creativity and visual memory.

■ Colour also allows you to introduce structure, weight and emphasis to your Mind Map.

■ Easy-flowing because you will want to be able to read what you have created and may want to write fast.

Are you sitting comfortably? Then we will begin.

■ Mini Mind Maps®

In order to warm up before embarking on a full-scale Mind Map, you may find it useful to do some quick brainstorming in the form of mini Mind Maps.

Identify Facts and Feelings: The simplest level of Mind Map represents a 'brainstorm' of emotions and ideas, such as Feelings and Facts. Remember the Change Mind Maps in Chapter 4? They can be used as a quick method for getting to the crux of an issue before you start focusing on the Big Picture.

Examine your choices: You can also create a simple 'Choice' Mind Map with your point of focus, i.e. your GOAL, in the centre, with two branches listed 'Action' and 'No Action'. (See Chapter 4.) This process is particularly powerful if you are temporarily stuck in a desire for 'No change'. It will remind you that Change is always the outcome; you are focusing on your Choice within that change.

In order to use Mind Maps to optimum effect as a transformative Tool for Change it is essential to combine the results of these mini Mind Maps in a larger thematic picture. The combined impact will encourage your brain to think more radiantly, more synergetically and more creatively about the future. You will be able to make Associations and see Connections in the branches of the Mind Map and catapult yourself towards seeing the Big Picture.

How to Mind Map®: the Big Picture

1. Thinking back to the Change Challenge on page 13, FOCUS again on your central aim, desire or vision. Be clear about what it is you are aiming or trying to resolve.

2. Turn your first sheet of paper SIDEWAYS [landscape], in order to start creating your Mind Map in the centre of the page. This will allow you freedom of expression, without being restricted by the narrow measure of the page.

3. Draw an IMAGE in the centre of the blank sheet of paper to represent your Change Challenge and draw an IMAGE that you associate with the change. Don't worry if you feel that you can't draw well; that doesn't matter. It is very important to use an image as the starting point for your Mind Map because an image is a visual reminder; it will jump-start your thinking by activating your imagination. You will automatically begin to think in a more creative and dynamic fashion. Your brain/ your memory will associate the image with the idea. The more images you use throughout the Mind Map, the more the visual impact on your brain/ your memory will be reinforced.

4. From the outset, use COLOUR for emphasis, structure, texture, creativity, and to add an element of fun to your thinking. This will stimulate your visual sense and reinforce the image in your mind. Use at least three colours and create your own colour-coding system. Colour can be used hierarchically, or thematically, or can be used to emphasize certain points.

5. Now draw a series of THICK LINES, radiating out from the centre of the image. These are the primary 'branches' of your Mind Map and will support your idea like the sturdy branches of a tree. It is important that you CONNECT the primary branches firmly to the central image, because the brain, and therefore the memory, operates by Association.

6. Make your lines CURVED rather than straight because they are more interesting to your eye and more memorable to your brain.

7. On each branch, write ONE KEY WORD that you associate with the change you are currently facing. These are your MAIN THOUGHTS about the Change Challenge.

    The branches could include key words such as:

SITUATION

FEELINGS

FACTS

CHOICES

Using only ONE KEY WORD per line allows you to define the very essence of the issue you are exploring and make the association more emphatically stored in the brain. Phrases and sentences limit the effect and confuse the memory.

8. Add a few EMPTY branches. Your brain will want to put something on them!

9. Next, create secondary level and third level branches for your related SECONDARY THOUGHTS and ASSOCIATED THOUGHTS. The secondary level connects to the primary branches, the third level to the secondary branches and so on. Connection is everything in this process. The words you choose for each of your branches can relate to anything that is concerning you at the moment. You may want to include branches that represent the WHO, WHAT, WHERE, WHY, HOW of the situation as well as the CONSEQUENCES of ACTION and NO ACTION and your CHOICES for change.

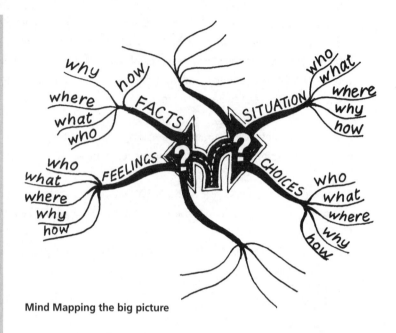

Mind Mapping the big picture

For a more detailed account of how to begin this process you may also find my earlier books, *The Mind Map Book* and *Use Your Head*, useful ready-reference tools.

Mind Mapping is a dynamic and exciting tool for planning smarter and faster. The creation of a Mind Map is a revolutionary way to tap into the infinite resources in your brain, to make appropriate decisions and to understand your feelings.

■ How to read Mind Maps

Assessing the Options: Once you have captured the results of your brain's creativity, use your imagination to consider your choices. The more you look at the situation in detail, the better prepared you will be and the more flexible you will be in tackling it. Be conscious of where you are in the TEFCAS process so that you can assess where you need to Check and Adjust this Feedback – and so that you can decide where the next Try will need to be.

First of all, imagine: what is the WORST that could happen? When? Where?

Fill in the words on this mini-Mind Map.

If ALL of this happened ... where would be the *good* in the situation?

Then, imagine: what is the BEST that could happen?

Fill in the words on this mini-Mind Map.

If ALL of this happened ... how could you improve it even more?

Remember: in every 'BAD' situation there is some 'GOOD'. There is also FASCINATING. The fascinating branch is neither 'Good' nor 'Bad' and includes observations, questions, wonderings, imaginings.

Mind Mapping to explore your situation and choices

Are the results looking interesting?

Now take a break! Listen to some music, go for a walk, talk to a friend. Do something that will stimulate your senses and allow your mind to assimilate the results of your work.

On your return, consider what has been useful in what you have done so far. Go back and look over all you have created and gathered. LOOK at the information as though you were weighing up another person's situation. What do you see? What strikes you?

Do you feel yourself saying 'Aha!' as things become clearer? We are usually better at seeing 'solutions' for others, so be the 'other' for yourself!

Weighting the results: If you are torn between different options for action, you will find it useful to 'weight' your answers by numbering them. This will enable you to assess your preferred plan of action with objectivity and clarity.

For example, if you have eight reasons for changing your situation and seven reasons for not changing your situation, the similarity of the result will create a dilemma.

However – if you *focus* your mind and *weight* each one of the reasons on a scale of 0–100 you will be able to see with more subtlety and clarity where the real drivers for change are occurring.

Continue this process with each of your reasons for change and reasons for non-change, until you have completed all branches of your Mind Map. Then add up the totals.

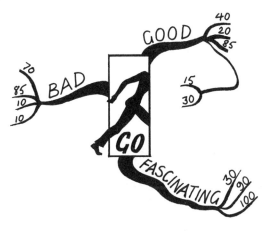

Weighting your options

In most instances you will find that there is a clear numerical advantage for one decision or the other. When this is the case, you make the decision to change. **This does NOT mean you *immediately* drop everything and make the change straight away!** What it does mean is that you have now decided on a new course of action in your life.

If you need to focus on a particular branch of the Mind Map in more detail, use the topic as the point of a new Mind Map, and begin the process again. The deeper you delve, the more connections and associations your brain will make.

Feeling stuck? Often we get stuck in Change Fear. We get too tired and down to be able to crawl out on top. When that happens, a smile or a laugh can change your outlook.

TAKE A BREAK.

Go and watch a comedy show/ have a laugh with a friend. Laughter boosts your serotonin levels and encourages your brain to think positive thoughts. The change in mood will enable you to view the ongoing change more positively and objectively.

■ How to apply Mind Maps®

Mind Maps can be used for absolutely anything in life. Once you have become used to using Mind Maps you will find that you use them intuitively to navigate your way through change. They will become an invaluable and indispensable part of your life, as the mini Mind Map following demonstrates.

A Mind Map of Change Mind Maps

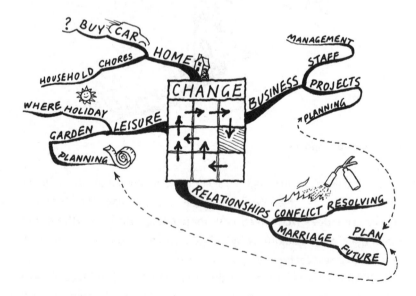

The following case study is a worked example showing how Mind Maps can be used to take definitive action to change your life path.

■ Mind Map®: The Job Change

Tom attended a Buzan Centre workshop when he had just turned 38 and was at a personal crossroads in his life. He had been working as a chartered surveyor since he qualified and although he had been offered partnership within the practice he was feeling unfulfilled at work and hungered for a change. He believed that once he turned 40 it would be too late to do anything different and so felt personal pressure to make a new start now. He had good relationships with his client contacts and every reason to believe he could successfully start his own business should he choose to. However, he was in a very negative frame of mind.

> **Change Check:** If you are thinking that you might want to change your job, it is conceivable that you may be deceiving yourself as to the true reasons for the change. The man or woman who is capable of TEFCAS and Meta-Positive Thinking will examine every reason he or she has for change and make sure that those reasons are honest and congruent with their beliefs.

At the time, Tom believed his motivation for change to be:

■ Ambition. To discover his true potential and to achieve financial success and personal fulfilment in his work.

■ Disillusionment. He no longer felt that his job was fulfilling. He was bored and wanted to be able to work on his own terms.

■ Financial. He worked hard and was good at what he did, but felt he wasn't paid enough.

■ Overwork. His workload was large, he worked very long hours, had no-one to delegate to and he found his bosses unapproachable. He didn't see this changing with the promotion.

■ Lack of recognition. He felt he had given the company a great deal over the years and believed he should have received both recognition and promotion at an earlier stage in his career.

In actual fact Tom's deep reasons for change were:

■ Financial difficulties. He was living beyond his means and was juggling debt.

- Overwork. He had been moonlighting in order to earn more money to pay off his credit cards and was constantly tired.
- Loss of confidence in his ability.
- Stress. His time management skills were weak and the senior partner was chiding him constantly as a result.
- Lack of balance. He worked hard and played hard with 'the lads' but was tired of being single and knew few people outside his profession.
- Poor health. He had given up sport completely in recent years and put on weight. He was beginning to feel tired all the time.
- Fear. He was terrified that accepting promotion would lead to failure.
- Wishful thinking. He had friends whose lives seem more balanced. He was convinced that everyone else was having more fun, was better off and happier than he was. He felt he 'needed a change' in order to 'reconnect with the true Tom'.

Tom's first Mind Map had at its centre an image of a pile of coins. He saw improving his financial situation as his primary Goal in moving jobs.

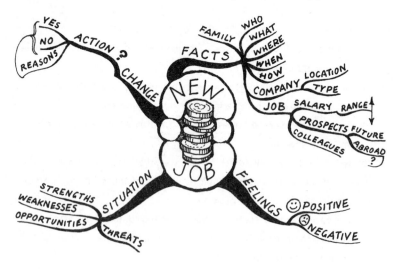

The process of personal exploration and focus led Tom to rediscover his personal strengths, and his enthusiasm for his profession. He realized that there were three different issues that required his focus:

■ The first was not his financial difficulties but more crucially the fact that his life was out of balance.

■ The second was his career, which he came to realize was not only on track, it was also where he wanted to be.

■ The third was his financial situation, which was the result of mismanagement rather than any innate misfortune.

Taking stock in this way helped Tom to face the Truth in his situation. He concluded that he had become stuck in a downward TEFCAS spiral and that he needed to stabilize his present situation before making any radical changes. Given the support of his current employers, who he could now see with objectivity were encouraging and supporting him, he decided to stay put, to plan for the long term and to revise his current life style – one step at a time.

Tom was a perfect example of someone tempted towards making an inappropriate and *radical* change – an *illusion* of progress – in order to avoid the Truth of the situation.

Two years further on, Tom has turned a corner in his life. After a number of false starts he has now adopted Mind Maps as a routine part of his life. This tool has enabled him not only to become more Focused in his daily actions, but also to incorporate Planning towards his medium- and long-term Goals a natural part of his life.

■ Reasons for change and reasons for not changing

A job or career change or starting a business venture are ideal opportunities for the use of a Mind Map. A Mind Map will allow you to see in one visual grasp all the reasons that are leading you towards a wish for change. You need to Mind Map all the reasons for changing, but to make sure that your change is appropriate and ultimately beneficial to you, you also need to Mind Map all the reasons for not changing. In examining those reasons, it is always essential to balance your considerations. Select the ones that are most appropriate and change your actions based on the best reasons for change.

Reasons for Change: One reason for considering whether to change your job, as in Tom's case, might be because you want a much more creative occupation. Your current job may be repetitive, non-demanding and dull. If you are a creative individual, this is a very, very important reason for change and you might weight this as 94 on a scale of 0–100.

Reasons for Not Changing: These might include the fact that you are receiving a very handsome wage for the monotonous task you are doing. If money is important to you, this is going to be a heavily weighted item. You might weigh it in at 90.

If you decide, having considered your weighted Mind Maps, to stay where you are, *all the same rules apply.*

The decision to stay where you are, in your current job, requires you to go through steps that are identical to those through which you went in deciding whether to *change* your job. You now know, as a positive Change Thinker and potential Change Maker, that staying where you are means that you *have* to change and that your current job *is* going to change. It is therefore extremely useful to realize that where you are *is* your new job.

Spend a few moments thinking about the undeniable truth that every second of your life is the beginning of the rest of your life.

Every second of your life is the beginning of the rest of your life; therefore every second in your current job is the beginning of a 'new' job. If you focus on making sure that your new job always remains fresh and exciting in your mind, you will be taking control of your destiny within that occupation.

Mind Maps become infinitely powerful when combined with awareness of the TEFCAS process. Applying TEFCAS and living though change consciously will allow you to Check every Trial at every stage of the Mind Map process; to look objectively at the resulting Events and gain Feedback from yourself and others; to Check your actions and reactions as you move ever onwards through ongoing Adjustment to create a series of Successes en route towards your ultimate, Mind Mapped, Goal.

■ Planning your future

In Chapter 9 of the book we will explore in more detail how Mind Maps can be used as a Tool for Planning your future and creating a personal Change

Journal that will capture your ideas and your ideals, and which will also act as a record of your life's transformational journey. At the heart of your journey, influencing your ability to succeed, is your personal Attitude. Your personal Attitude is a crucial factor that determines whether you achieve positive or negative Success. That is why Attitude is the next Buzan step for influencing personal change. In the next chapter, however, we will explore first, the extent to which your personal Attitude is at the heart of your ability to Succeed in your ambitions.

Change your thoughts and you change your world.

Norman Vincent Peale

Chapter 7
Choosing your future

❏ Attitude and choice

❏ Buzan's Tools for Transformation: 5. Meta-Positive Thinking

❏ Create Meta-Positive thinking statements

❏ Transform the negative voice of change to the positive voice of change

Wherever there is change, there is choice. Your attitude to change is linked, inevitably, to that choice. You have the power to choose how you decide to arrive at change. You have the ability to deal with whatever it is you are currently facing and living through, as well as planning effectively, step by step, for an empowered future.

■ Where are you now?

Negative (Reactive)	Positive (Proactive)
If you are reactive you feel as though:	*If you are proactive you feel as though:*
You have NO choice	You have a goal, vision & purpose
You have NO control	You have a burning desire to make that goal a reality
It is out of your hands	You are unstoppable
It will never end	You are unbeatable
'They' are wearing you down	You have limitless resources
You hate every moment	You WILL find a way!
You have no energy	You are FULL of energy!
You are wrung out	You are inspired
You are stressed to the max	You are in control
You don't want to face another day	Each day is a gift

Are you more strongly biased towards one set of reactions than the other? This chapter will revolutionize the way you think forever. Even if you are dipping into the negative list at the moment, you will relate only to the characteristics on the positive list by the time you have applied the principles from this chapter.

I will be encouraging you to revisit the CTQ on pages 47–51 when you have completed this section and to revise your answers if you feel your attitude has changed on any points.

From time to time life will throw up changes that are instantaneous. These changes will be perceived as either positive or negative depending upon our personal approach to that change and whether it is Enforced, Advised, Natural or Anticipated, as previously discussed in Chapter 4. How well we assimilate and learn from these experiences comes down to Attitude and Self-Esteem. Both of these are driven by our self-talk – the way in which we talk to our innermost selves. An example of this is shown in the stories of two different people each with a similar injury to their dominant hand.

■ A handy tale

Mike and Terry met in hospital in 2001. Each had severely damaged their right, dominant hands in separate accidents. Terry had become extremely depressed by the experience, and continually complained about how difficult it was because he couldn't carry on in the way he had before. 'Everything had changed' to make life more difficult for him. He was 'unlucky'; it 'wasn't fair'. He was dejected and unappreciative of his carers and became solitary and introverted. During every second of every day he was a real 'pain' and became increasingly frustrated.

Mike, on the other hand (if you'll pardon the pun!), looked upon his injury as a challenge and with an element of humour. He told people that he had been given the great opportunity of developing his non-dominant hand in order to become more ambidextrous and therefore more physically balanced. He took this challenge seriously, and during his convalescence from work set about training his non-dominant hand in skills such as writing, carrying, cooking and so on. He used the time to relax and to be more sociable. To add spice to the whole experience he also took up art. By the time his injury had repaired, he was a refreshed and changed individual who had used a cataclysmic change to transform his manual and physical skills.

Our 'unlucky' victim Terry emerged from his convalescence also changed – into someone who had become frustrated and bitter and who felt that three months of his life had been wasted. Sadly, he was right – but only because he chose to waste them.

■ Nurturing your inner voice of change

The pessimist sees difficulty in every opportunity.
The optimist sees opportunity in every difficulty.
Winston Churchill

Each of us has an inner Voice of Change that chatters away to the brain incessantly, day in day out, week in week out, like a fitness coach training an athlete. The voice tells the brain how to think and what to do; it judges our every move and phrase. It dictates whether we will act as a Positive Change Thinker or a Negative Change Thinker. Even though we may not pause to listen consciously – through prayer, meditation, daydreaming, imagination or visualization – we still hear and respond to everything the Voice of Change says to us. We listen with equal attention whether the inner voice encourages us to think positive or negative thoughts.

The *Positive* Voice of Change says that each individual has responsibility for their own lives, and the freedom to choose their response to any given situation. The Positive Voice encourages the Change Thinker to work *with* the Universe to bring about change and use his or her personal Circle of Influence to influence the world for the better.

The Positive Voice of Change will by definition tend to focus on the positive, whatever the situation. When something goes wrong, it will encourage the Change Thinker to look for a solution, prompting a 'can do' attitude that will assume a positive outcome is possible – eventually.

The Positive Voice of Change will make sure that:

- The things you say to yourself are personal and relating to your essence.
- You have *real* goals, that are obtainable without being ridiculously easy.
- Everything you say to yourself will be Truthful and will give you the impetus and drive to motivate you towards a change you wish for.
- What you say to yourself is anchored in the present, and will propel you into the future.
- This will give you confidence, harmony, balance and strength.
- It provides you with instructions that are *comprehensively* beneficial to you.
- Everything that is infused into your brain will be attractive to you, will *draw you towards it,* as any positive goal will.
- Everything that is fed into your brain will be positive, accurate, truthful, clear, concise and crystalline – like an injection of energy.

Having done all of this, the Positive Voice of Change will be *guaranteeing* that your vision is large, totally focused and directed towards something to which you will be enthusiastically and inevitably drawn.

There is also a Negative Voice of Change, however, that speaks with a different motive. The Negative Voice is the Positive Voice's *Doppelgänger*, or alter ego. In extreme, the Negative Voice of Change encourages the Change Thinker to believe him or herself to be a victim of circumstance, to take a fatalistic approach to life, to believe that the universe is conspiring against them, giving them trials over which they have no control. The Change Thinker who listens to the Negative Voice of Change will feel out of control of his or her personal situation, will say that they have *no choice*, and that there is therefore no possibility to bring about personal change, even in as tiny a circle of influence as him or her self.

The Negative Voice of Change will feed a negative attitude and tend to focus on negatives within the environment. When something has gone wrong, the Negative Voice is likely to encourage the Change Thinker to give in to his or her emotions, whether anger, moodiness, tearfulness, aggression or resignation; to automatically begin to search for other things that can go wrong and end up saying things like, 'It's unfair, why does it always happen to *me*?' or 'I'm such a bad person, I deserve this to happen' – neither of which is true.

At different times of your life you will have different responses to different events because your Positive and Negative Voices of Change live within and influence the same brain and the same body. One voice directs you to be like a dolphin in an ocean, navigating the currents and the eddies by choice, the other voice encourages you to opt to drift along like a plankton, at the total will of the shifting tides.

A Native American elder once described his own inner struggles in this manner: 'Inside of me there are two dogs. One of the dogs is mean and evil. The other dog is good. The mean dog fights the good dog all the time.' When asked which dog wins, he reflected for a moment and replied, 'The one I feed the most.'

The key to transforming the self-talk of the Negative Voice of Change into the self-talk of the Positive Voice of Change is *Meta-Positive* Thinking.

■ The power of Meta-Positive Thinking

> *We do not see things as they are; we see things as we are.*
> **Talmud**

Meta-Positive Thinking is based around self-talk techniques that are central to focusing on your Goal or your Vision in a positive way in order to achieve your aims and ambitions. Changing your thinking to Meta-Positive Thinking will enable you to combat any negative self-talk that has accumulated over the years and may be currently distracting you from achieving your goals.

The key to Meta-Positive Thinking is the ability to identify what is and what is not within your immediate sphere of influence; to recognize what you can and what you cannot change in the short term. You will then be able to focus with clarity on that area of the situation where you *do* or *can* have immediate influence.

■ Changing perspective

If you feel that 95 per cent of your situation is non-negotiable, unavoidable, absolutely cannot be changed, then focus on the 5 per cent that you feel *can* be changed.

It is easier to feel motivated to push forward from within the 5 per cent place than to feel trapped within the 95 per cent place.

In fact, unless you are faced with a natural or physical change that is irreversible – such as death, or losing a limb – the chances are that 95 per cent of the situation CAN be changed. It is a matter of changing perspective.

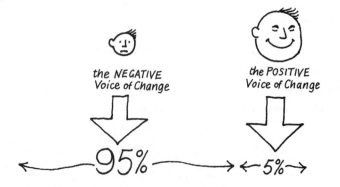

the NEGATIVE
Voice of Change

the POSITIVE
Voice of Change

←——— 95% ———→ ←5%→

This means working positively to transform your situation from within.

If you are already an ambitious Change Thinker and Change Maker who wants to reach even greater levels of personal success, Meta-Positive Thinking will ensure that you reach your optimum capacity for personal achievement.

If you are stuck in your personal '95%' and want to expand your '5%' capacity for positive change, read on ...

Buzan's Tools for Transformation
Meta-Positive Thinking

There are eight steps to achieving Meta-Positive Thinking, which, from the very *moment* you start to follow them, will allow your ever-transforming brain cells to let go of the shackles of past negative behaviours and begin to enhance your positive qualities.

Step One: Make the decision to change
Step Two: Clarify your Vision
Step Three: Establish a Meta-Positive Attitude
Step Four: Shape up your brain for Meta-Positive Fitness
Step Five: The Truth Principle
Step Six: Repetition
Step Seven: One step at a time
Step Eight: Commitment

■ Step One: Make the decision to change

If you wish to change, you are already a positive thinker and have the potential to become a Meta-Positive Thinker. You have already decided that your current situation needs improvement or requires you to be extra positive, and you have the desire and are motivated to change from your current state towards the envisioned state.

Step Two: Clarify your Vision

Every Goal begins with a Vision. If you think positively in the appropriate way, you will give energy to that vision, and *increase the probability* that you will bring all your mental and physical forces in alignment in order to achieve it. Over time you will *change your behaviour* to give added impetus to the direction you are already going in, or will change direction in a *new and positive way*. Remember:

Wanting is a dream with no direction.

If you 'want' something, the only way of achieving it is to focus on it and to decide what TEFCAS steps are needed in order to progress towards that Vision. If you don't plan, the distance between wanting and achieving will never get any smaller.

One of the great accomplishments of the good Change Thinker is to keep the Vision alive, despite negative influences that may surround it, despite the demands on time that may try to drag you away from it.

Step Three: Establish a Meta-Positive Attitude

In order to bring about positive change you must think in such a way as to *oblige*, rather than force, your brain to become the optimum agent for positive change, and to do what you ask it to do.

Your goal must be totally positive. Your Meta-Positive thinking statement must be totally accurate and direct you towards the desired positive outcome.

The brain that is not organized, that is not congruent, that is not disciplined or focused, may become 'stuck' in fuzzy thinking or change in ways you do not wish it to be changed. So in order to oblige your brain to respond and change in a positive direction, you have to give it the right instructions. You must become Meta-Positive in your thinking.

Meta-Positive Thinking statements must be:

Personal — Statements need to begin with 'I'

Stated in the present — Statements must include the phrase 'I am', and be stated in the present tense. **Beware** of substituting 'I will', 'I shall', 'I intend', 'I plan to' all of which offer a future promise that may never be fulfilled.

Stated as a process — Statements must be active in order to be motivational, and must therefore include a verb ending in 'ing'. Beware of using phrases such as 'I am thinking of' or 'I am going to', which express future intent rather than present action.

Real — Statements must be related directly to your current situation and to what is actually happening in your life.

Obtainable — Statements need to reflect a target that is neither too easy to obtain nor too difficult; it must be realistic and obtainable.

Motivational — Statements must be proactive and focus on what you DO want to achieve. They must not include reference to anything you are trying to avoid.

Relevant — Statements must relate directly to your current situation, rather than abstract ideals.

Truthful — Your brain is a truth-seeking mechanism and will know if your statement is based on a lie. Make sure your statement is 100 per cent true and achievable.

Beneficial — Statements need to reflect an achievement that is of true benefit to you in order to gain your commitment.

Attractive — Statements need to conjure up a pleasant image, rather than one of suffering or deprivation. Aversion therapy rarely works.

Positively directed — Your statement must be totally positive and directed towards your goal.

Accurate	Your statement must direct you towards your desired outcome.
Vision	Your statement must direct your mind towards a vision (a clear image) that is positive.
Repeated	Your statement must be repeated regularly in order for the brain to adjust its behaviour and change negative habits of the past into positive habits of the present.

Meta-Positive Thinking represents Structure and Measurability – a process which defines the steps and in which the actions and the results of the actions are measurable.

Beware of the traits of meta-negative statements which will ensure the opposite, that:

■ Your goals are impersonal.

■ Your goals are unreal.

■ Your goals are unobtainable.

■ The phrases you use provide you with no motivation.

■ Your thinking directs you only into the past or the present.

■ The things you repeat to yourself are not directly relevant to your goal.

■ The processes by which you go from A to B will have no structure and no measurability.

■ The things you say to yourself will conceal subtle lies.

■ Similarly, they will conceal subtle poisons or dangers to your system.

■ Under the guise of 'goodness' they will encourage you to say things that are deeply unattractive to you, that are falsely positive, but truly negative.

■ You will feed words into your brain that are fuzzy at the edges and will becloud and befog the issue.

■ Step Four: Shape up your brain for Meta-Positive Fitness

Does your Inner Voice of Change motivate you to deliver positive results, or do you often feel demotivated, inadequate and doomed to failure? Is your Inner Voice of Change making you a Positive Change Thinker or a Negative

Change Thinker? Do the things that your Inner Voice of Change says move you towards your goal – or further away from it? The differences can be subtle and can vary wildly during the course of a project.

Many positive thinking schools of thought are attractive. In reality they often contain mazes, misleading paths and in some cases opposite directions to the goal. It is therefore essential for the Change Thinker to learn the correct formula for bringing about progressive change towards the direction desired.

To illustrate how Meta-Positive Thinking works and how you can transform your Inner Voice of Change, I am going to introduce you to two characters. You may well have met them previously in your life, and their voices will be familiar to you.

The Positive Voice of Change is **Victor**, the Change Maker. Victor is directed purely towards coaching you on how to become a Positive Change Thinker.

The Negative Voice of Change is **Vic**, the Victim of Circumstance. Vic is directed purely towards coaching you on how to become a Negative Change Thinker.

Vic and Victor are Inner Voices of Change who in this scenario are aiding our budding Change Maker [You] to Stop Smoking.

These principles can be applied to anything, from developing confident presentation skills, to deciding to run your own business, to planning a project, to organizing a wedding, to turning your life around following a divorce or other personal crisis.

Vic and Victor have quite different approaches to influencing your thoughts and actions. Consider which Voice of Change is currently accompanying you on your journey.

Just as in sport some coaches are very bad and some are really magnificent, so too we have very bad and truly magnificent Voices of Change. We are going to compare their styles.

Introducing Vic, the Victim of Circumstance

Vic is your Inner Negative Voice of Change. He can be superficially charming, and often tells you what you want to hear, but has a tendency to play the 'blame' game and can become a bully if you make mistakes. He talks to you about the problems associated with smoking because he is worried about your health. He tends to refer everything back to his own experiences and says he knows you can give up as he's done it many times himself! He will also nag and tell you not to be so weak if you are tempted to smoke. This can crescendo on occasion and he is apt to tell you that you're useless, hopeless and that you'll never succeed.

You forgive him because you feel that he is right. If he has been playing the blame game too much, however, his company will get you down, and you will find yourself thinking about smoking even more as a result of talking to him.

Ultimately Vic has low self-esteem and doesn't really believe he can help you to change, so he doesn't take his responsibility seriously and will blame you for your non-achievement. He doesn't really *want* you to change because he will have lost a familiar companion. There is therefore another side to his character that will deliberately try to tempt you from your path.

Be warned – he is also a master of disguise and has developed a compelling Victor impersonation over the years. The true Change Thinker can always tell the difference between them, however, because Vic is unfocused and his changes motivate you *away* from achieving your true goal.

Vic is concerned about your self-regard. He will encourage you to say in pursuit of your goal of change such things as 'I am a wonderful person'. This is all very well, but it does not add any weight or impetus to the probability that you will change your behaviour. It is equivalent to saying 'The sky is blue'. Yes, the sky is blue, and yes, you are a nice person, and … *yes, you can carry on smoking*. Such directions give you *no* direction.

In saying such things as 'you can break the habit', Vic is offering false encouragement. The sentiment is encouraging, but the statement is not grounded in the present. In order to become real, the statement needs to provide motivation relating to starting *now*, this moment.

Victor, the Positive Voice of Change, will realize that what you need to say to yourself must be relevant to the goal that you have in mind.

Vic as your Voice of Change is assisted by misconceptions such as 'No pain, no gain' and 'In order to succeed, you must suffer'. Of course we learn through suffering, and many books have been written on the subject; in general, however, the main lesson that we learn is to avoid it at all costs.

Suffering is not the natural goal of the human brain. If it were, we would all be extinct.

Victor, on the other hand, is aware that the most beneficial methods for bringing about change are the ones that offer rewards for appropriate behaviour. The Negative Voice of Change will, by definition, focus on the negative. Vic instructs you to *stop doing what you don't want to do*. In other words he focuses your attention on the thing you want to stop doing.

For example, by telling you constantly to 'Stop **Smoking**', the word 'smoking' immediately conjures up the sight, smell and desire for a cigarette. In other words, if you keep thinking about stopping *smoking*, you are unlikely to focus on the word 'stopping'. What you are *actually* doing is thinking about smoking, and if you keep thinking about smoking ... *you will want to smoke even more*.

His choice of language will force you to focus on and therefore reinforce your negative behaviour.

Introducing Victor, the Change Thinker

Victor is your Inner *Positive* Voice of Change. He is an explorer who has combated many obstacles and has achieved many goals. Victor points you constantly towards your Vision; he will take you into the future in the direction of where you wish to go.

Victor may seem a somewhat distant figure to begin with: a high-achiever, self-assured, calm with self-confidence. You are not sure initially whether you can match up to him or his expectations; however, you discover that Victor is approachable, with an astute sense of humour and entirely focused on ensuring you achieve your goal. He doesn't immediately reach out to rescue you, but stands back and helps you to identify where you went wrong and what you might do differently next time. He always seems to be there for you – he never chastises, he's always grounded, always tells you 'like it is' and you want to earn his respect.

Victor doesn't want you to be dependent upon him; he wants you to make changes for yourself. He has high self-esteem and he wants you to be his equal, to offer him new challenges in the future, to be your partner in achieving ever-greater goals.

Vic's key phrases include:

You are a *wonderful* person.

You *can* break the habit.

No pain, no gain!

Don't keep talking about stopping smoking. Just stop.

You're hopeless. You'll never quit smoking.

Your mind's response is:

So what? It hasn't helped me to stop smoking. Pass me another cigarette.

I really want to. I'll have my last cigarette right now.

Ouch! I'd rather have a cigarette!

I know you're right, I really should. I really will. Soon … Another cigarette, please.

I know, I'm useless. I may as well have another cigarette as I'm going to fail anyway.

Look back at the points on pages 119–20. You will see that none of these statements meets the requirements of a Meta-Positive Thinking statement. In fact, they are opposite to a Meta-Positive Thinking statement and, worse, will spiral your brain into a Meta-Negative response.

The Positive Voice of Change directs you *towards* positive *change* rather than encouraging you constantly to look backwards at your habit. Victor does not mention the word 'smoking', because he knows that the more you think about the things you are trying to move away from, the more you will change towards *un*-changing. He wants your meta-positive thoughts to become stronger than your meta-negative thoughts.

In truth, Vic has it within himself to be a Victor – and to be victorious over himself, but at present he has adopted the role of victim of circumstance and believes the world is against him. He is not being honest with himself and so at present is stuck in his never-ending cycle of non-change and negative repetition.

Victor's key phrases are:	Your mind's response is:
You are becoming healthier.	*I feel healthier and I am succeeding in my efforts.*
You are getting closer to your goal.	*I am succeeding and so am I motivated to continue.*
You are developing the right attitude.	*I am feeling positive and confident in my ability to succeed.*
You are looking more attractive.	*I like the improvement and I am continuing in my positive new habit.*

These statements tally with all the requirements of Meta-Positive Thinking statements as listed on page 119.

■ Step Five: The Truth Principle

The brain is a truth-seeking mechanism that can tell when you are lying to yourself. It is therefore extremely important, when developing Meta-Positive Thinking, to make quite sure that the things you are saying to yourself are not in fact subtly negative lies.

Vic and Victor above demonstrated the differences. With the best of intentions, Vic will lie to you, and encourage you to lie to yourself. He will encourage you to tell yourself that you *don't like* smoking or that you prefer eating celery to smoking. The problem is that you know this is unlikely to be true. What will you need to do in such a situation? *Have another cigarette!*

Victor realizes that such things are lies and will encourage you always to tell yourself the Truth. The fact that you like smoking is both understandable and acceptable. Victor will encourage you to realize that you are clever enough to realize this and to realize that, although smoking is enjoyable, it is also on many levels harmful. Being a Change Thinker he knows that you have the capacity to change the habit by looking at the 'big picture' and focusing on other benefits.

Vic is a scaremonger. As a Negative Voice of Change he will whisper in your ear that if you keep smoking you will suffer from emphysema, you will be weak, you will have no stamina, you will be increasingly sick, and there is an increased possibility of dying from the results of a heart attack, stroke or cancer and suffering from arthritis.

Think about what he is filling your mind with: horrifying truths, negative images, minute by minute, day in, day out. Such a Voice of Change is like a tireless garbage truck, constantly dumping refuse into your mind. The result of such coaching is that you will become stressed, fearful, tense, depressed, defeatist, will feel disempowered, and your self-confidence will decrease. What will our smoker need to do in such a situation? Reach for the comfort of another cigarette!

Victor the Change Maker, as your Positive Voice of Change, will inform you of all the wonderful benefits of engaging in behaviours that bring you pleasure, sensual satisfaction, enjoyment, fun and *health*. He realizes that your brain is far more motivated by and attracted to positive reward than negative punishment. Your positive Voice of Change also realizes that this creates in your body and immune system a far healthier state of being.

■ Step Six: Repetition

Your Inner Voice of Change is speaking to you right NOW. It is speaking to you constantly, to encourage you constantly, to guide you constantly, so you need to be conscious of what your inner Voice of Change is saying, you need to pay attention to the *real* message, in order to help it say the correct things to you.

You were born to be a positive Change Maker even though you may feel on occasion that you are a Victim of Circumstance. If your inner voice stays positive and you choose to use Meta-Positive Thinking methods and phrases effectively, constantly, and with conviction, you will permanently transform the voice of 'Vic' into the Meta-Positive voice of Change Maker 'Victor'.

Remember the value of repetition.

Repetition increases the probability of repetition.
This means that more you repeat your Meta-Positive Thinking
phrases, the more you will succeed in progressing towards achieving
your ultimate goal.

■ Step Seven: One Step at a Time

The good Change Thinker realizes that change by definition has to take place one step at a time and that *The First Step is a Very Important Step.*

Your first step *must* be based on a proper assessment of your position and the full situation in order to establish appropriate goals, and appropriate procedures for getting to those envisioned goals.

Step Seven therefore works in partnership with Step One. You must be clear about what your goal is in order to move towards it and you must COMMIT to taking that step.

You must know where you are in order to take the first step. If you don't know where you are, you could be anywhere, and your first step could lead you right over the cliff, right into the swamp, or could be just a virtual step, which has no reality.

■ Step Eight: Commitment

Until one is committed, there is hesitancy, the chance to draw back,
always ineffectiveness. Concerning all acts of initiative (and cre-
ation), there is one elementary truth the ignorance of which kills
countless ideas and splendid plans: that the moment one definitely
commits oneself, then providence moves too. All sorts of things
occur to help one that would never otherwise have occurred. A
whole stream of events issues from the decision, raising in one's
favour all manner of unforeseen incidents and meetings and material
assistance, which no man could have dreamed would have come his
way. Whatever you can do or dream you can, begin it. Boldness has
genius, power and magic in it. Begin it now.
(Anon. Thought to be inspired by Johann Wolfgang von Goethe)

To begin with, your Negative Voice of Change will seem louder than your Positive Voice of Change. This is not really surprising as your Positive Voice is still relatively young and inexperienced. The more *committed* you are to achieving the task, and the more you repeat positive phrases to yourself, and the more you repeat the positive change patterns, the greater will be the likelihood of further positive repetition. To begin with, commit to a minimum of five positive repetitions per day. You will be amazed at how soon the Meta-Positive Voice speaks louder than the Meta-Negative Voice and at how readily you are able to change for the better.

■ Self-talk challenges and temptations: a fable

Consider your mind to be like a giant physical territory – your Thinking Terrain – offering many challenges. In order to achieve your goal of changing the habit of negative thinking into Meta-Positive Thinking, you need to review the terrain, assess where the obstacles are, decide on a route to achieve your objective and travel prepared to combat challenges on the way. The terrain is demanding, but capable of amazing transformation.

This fable explores what happens when you are asked to make a major presentation. You are initially terrified – of making a fool of yourself, of forgetting your words, of not being heard, of doing a bad job.

Vic's Voice of Change rings loudly and negatively in your head:
■ I'm hopeless at speaking in public.
■ I remember the last time I had to give a talk. I forgot my words.
■ Everyone else who speaks will be better than me.
■ I'm no good at holding the audience.
■ There is an awful lot at stake here and I'm going to make a fool of myself.
■ I'm petrified!

You immediately combat the negativity with the positive voice of Victor using Meta-Positive Thinking:
■ I am improving my presentation skills.
■ I am preparing a Mind Map so I will be able to recall everything I need to say.

■ I am researching the subject.

■ I am planning ahead because I have learned from my past experience.

■ I am asking friends to help me rehearse.

■ I am scheduling my preparation so that I will perform to the best of my ability.

■ I am courageous and am going to rise to the occasion.

Mission accomplished? Not quite.

Vic is a master of disguise, and in spite of Victor's best efforts, Vic will continue to crop up just when you least want him to during the next few weeks.

During the course of your preparation there will be mountains of self-doubt to conquer, swamps of panic and quicksand to take you unawares, mazes of disorganization to get lost in, trails of information in all directions, and hazards of all kinds. Similarly you know that there are streams of confidence to refresh yourself and drink from, there are fruits of knowledge on the trees, there is the food of friendship to sustain you, adventures to be had and new experiences to enjoy; there will be fine weather to rejuvenate you and all kinds of environmental stimulus to help propel you on your way. You know too that with careful planning, you will be enriched and strengthened by the experience.

Beware of the quicksand!

One of the areas of quicksand in developing Meta-Positive Thinking is that in weaker moments you can easily slip into the false assumption that listening to the negative Voice of Change is *easier* because it is familiar and apparently requires less effort. You may find yourself thinking that you don't *really* have to change, that things are fine as they are.

Whenever this thought rears its not-so-pretty head, you need to realize, as you must always realize, that when you take the decision *not* to change, you *are* changing anyway. You are reinforcing the very behaviour that you want to change.

The false trail of self-interest

Vic will lead you into a false sense of confidence by enticing you with statements which tell you: 'You can do what you want to do, when you choose to do it – so why not go out for a drink with your friends this evening, and delegate the research for your talk to someone else?'

If you can do what you want to do, then of course you can do anything, which may include continuing to perform badly at presentations. These insidious, invidious suggestions give you no motivation. They leave you without a mental compass.

The vow of Vision

Victor will counter self-interest by encouraging you to keep the Vision in your sights and to schedule your next point of action in a realistic timeframe.

'In order to make an excellent job of this I am going to get ahead of the game and Mind Map my plan of action after my four o'clock meeting this afternoon.'

The cobra of complacency

Vic in this form persuades you that you have already succeeded in making the decision to plan ahead, and you have a whole month yet – so:

'You don't *need* to start preparing today, do you? There is always tomorrow (and tomorrow and tomorrow…)'

The fire of focus

Victor, on the other hand, will be ready to combat complacency with the fire of focus and will always give you positive and motivational statements that oblige you to be directive, and insist that you become proactive. In other words, that you move from the state you are currently in towards your change goal.

'I am researching at the moment and am scheduled to complete this stage by midday on Friday. I am confident that I will achieve that, and can enjoy time with friends on Saturday afternoon.'

The whirlpool of wishful thinking

Vic will next try to entice you into a whirlpool which leads you into a constant spin, getting you nowhere nearer your goal at all, and in time farther and farther away from it even though you are spinning in the same current.

'I wish I didn't have to prepare for this presentation, I wish I knew what to say, I wish it was all over, I wish I could afford to go on holiday, I wish I could be at home playing with the children, I wish I was better at speaking in public, I wish ...'

The negative Voice of Change here encourages you to say to yourself that you want to have, or want to be, whatever it is, without taking appropriate steps to get there, and without changing your negative thinking habit.

The sirens of self-delusion

If you embrace this false goal and are enticed by the siren's songs you will be trapped forever in the whirlpool of wishful thinking. The infinite capacity of your brain enables you to want anything or indeed everything.

The Meta-Positive Thinker is fully aware of the siren's songs and is as attracted to them as everybody else. The difference is that the Meta-Positive Thinker, being aware that wishful thinking is a fantasy and a refuge, is capable of both listening to the song and maintaining the voyage to the goal, rather than giving in to the momentary delights of the sirens' seductions. He is not deaf; on the contrary, he is even more fully aware than most. His awareness enables him to appreciate the beauty of the songs, while realizing the trap that lies therein. The attraction of the Meta-Positive Thinker's grand Vision has much greater gravitational pull than the minor momentary song of the siren.

To bring about proactive change, you *must* develop self-management skills and your wishful thinking *must* be given direction. The Positive Voice of Change will encourage you to realize that wishful thinking – the *want* to *have* something, *do* something, or *achieve* something – can be transformed from a non-active state into a directed state, thus becoming a properly envisioned goal, with the energy of direction behind it.

'When I have completed the first draft I will take a half-hour break and see how much I would need to save up to take a holiday with the children. It will be fun to discuss our options when I get home this evening. It is useful to have this time to focus uninterrupted on my work.'

The promise of paradise

The next major Temptation is the promise of Paradise *at some time in the future*. Vic will encourage you to say that you *will* improve; that you *will* get better; that you *will* improve your attitude towards yourself and your physical health. This all sounds wonderful, and is extremely inviting. The problem with this kind of thinking is that, like the previous siren songs, it actually, and subtly, takes you away from the immediate reality of taking active steps towards achieving your Vision.

'I will practise this presentation again later in the week. I know I will be fine on the day and I'm sure we will win the business as a result. I will ask for a pay rise if that happens.'

The gift of the present

Victor will be ready to counter this attack with a reminder of the Gift of the Present. He will help you to realize that this is one of the ultimate traps, one of the ultimate chasms into which you can plunge. For if you keep coaching yourself that you *will*, you are constantly and eternally putting the necessity for action off into some undefined, obscure, unclear, hazy, misty point in the future; that gap between the present in which you now exist and that undefined future point of action can remain the same distance for a very, very long time. Every time you get to that point in the future, Vic will insist that you will repeat once again, that you *will [at some point]*, and in so saying, unwittingly you will be driven further towards the chasm's edge. For you will be eternally putting off the moment at which you have to act in order to bring about change.

Victor will coax you back from the abyss by encouraging you to repeat things to yourself that start in the present.

'I am rehearsing my presentation with colleagues today, and will have time to make revisions as a result. I am discussing my options for promotion this week with a commitment to sign a revised contract if we secure a deal with our client.'

Living in the moment

One of the traps of 'living in the moment' is that western thinkers often apply analytical thought to something that is far more strategic and consensual.

The Great Change Agent will be able to live in the moment while being simultaneously able to perceive all of memory and history, and simultaneously projecting into the future.

Living in the moment therefore becomes living in eternity.

The moment is not, as has been mistakenly assumed, a singular pinpoint in time. The moment is universal, encompassing the past, the present and the future.

Death by denial of self

Vic ultimately will encourage you to deny who you are; he will encourage you to say you are fit when you are not; that you are healthy when you are not; that you are happy when you are not; that you are successful when you are not. The smooth voice of the negative Change Agent is giving you a large, fat, sugar-coated, poisoned pill: he is telling you that you must *Live the Lie*.

'I may not be very good at presenting, but my clients like me, so I should be able to pull this deal off. I don't think it's a very good idea to be too corporate about these things anyway. It puts people off.'

The triumph of truth

The Positive Voice of Change will once again bring in the brain principle of *Truth*, and ask you to assess who you are objectively. Then, having established the current, relevant and truthful parameters, you can make sensible decisions about where you are and therefore what process you are going to use to get you to where you wish to go. You cannot get to where you wish to go if you don't know where you are – i.e. if you don't know your starting point for change.

'It was useful to gain the feedback when I rehearsed my talk this week. I can see what I need to do to make improvements. It's important that my presentation is informative without being overly formal.'

Needless to say it is the Positive Voice of Change using Meta-Positive Thinking techniques that will win the business on the day – and be relaxed and confident enough to enjoy a fortnight's holiday afterwards!

■ Meta-Positive Thinking in Practice

If we don't change our direction, we're likely to end up where we're headed.

Chinese Proverb

Bringing about change requires as much finesse, as much elegance and as much planning as it took to land *Beagle 2* on Mars. That whole fabulous exploration was a matter of bringing about phenomenal change. Everything about it concerned dealing with and working with change. Minerals were transformed into design materials, designs were interpreted and created into spaceships, rovers and balloons. The trajectory of Mars was estimated in relation to the trajectory of Earth; changes that were going to take place in the universe had to be calculated in relation to the changes that would take place on the Earth in order to transport the spaceship to Mars in precise fashion.

The Change process was envisioned, planned and executed to precision in order to bring about the realization of the goal.

If you have dreams and ambitions that you 'think about', 'are going to', 'intend to', 'mean to' put into action, consider for a moment what life could be like had some of the world's greatest inventors not pursued their Vision.

■ If Johannes Gutenberg had not developed the printing press.
■ If Copernicus had not proven that the world was round not the centre of the universe.
■ If Alexander Graham Bell had not invented the telephone.
■ If Michael Faraday had not discovered how to harness the power of electricity.
■ If Joseph Lister had not discovered the importance of antiseptic procedures in surgical medicine.

The world would be a radically different and profoundly poorer place.

We lead such busy and demanding lives that there are always compelling reasons for delaying or possibly never bringing about the changes we desire. The Change Thinker who remains a Thinker is different from one who becomes a Change Maker in one aspect only. Those who decide that they 'can do' things, have the same thoughts, but plan their future; they have the same desires, but use their desires as the impetus for action; they have the same fears, but use those fears as a motivation to bring about change.

▓ Meta-Positive Thinking and your Vision

Two of the greatest inhibitors to bringing about positive change are Stress and its accompanying twin companion, Fear: fear of consequences, fear of being made to look a fool, fear of the risk, fear of failure. All of these responses lead to negative changes in your brain-and-body system. They have a dramatic impact on the immune system, inhibiting its natural function, inducing shallow breathing, resulting in more constricted blood vessels.

To overcome the fear of going for it, you simply have to Try, but to try without knowing where you are headed means you are focused on the stress *instead* of the Goal. The most effective way to overcome stress is to focus afresh on your Vision (see Chapter 4).

Trying under stress produces a static mind and body that can lead to a sense of panic and inertia; this produces a rigidity of approach, which increases the probability of negative change or 'drowning' in events. To reverse that process it is always a matter of revisiting your Goal and what it is you need to do to bring about the desired change.

Don't try to do this on your own. Think about your personal support network. Who is there in your personal support group who can motivate you, guide you, share expert knowledge, give you TEFCAS Feedback?

If you were being swept away by the tide of that river, wouldn't you shout out and grab the lifeline that was thrown from the water's edge? Your daily life is no different, and if you are fearful or under pressure, the chances are that a new perspective will help you to see a new path to reaching your goal.

▓ Your Goal vs other people's

Stress and fear can result if you are being coerced into focusing on the achievement of someone else's goal instead of your own, or if you are focusing on something over which you have limited influence and no control. If you are dealing solely with the Change Goals of others you may literally be losing yourself.

How different it will feel if you are a willing partner in reaching a shared goal, or you are supporting someone you respect in the achievement of a goal with which you agree. The level of stress or fear increases if the goal you are pursuing is not congruent with your own desires.

It is important when you are seeking change, embarking on self-development, self-improvement, or involving yourself in a new task, that you make sure you have your own identity clearly established. Take time to take stock of your talents and what motivates you in life. If you understand your own strengths and weaknesses, you are better placed to help yourself and others bring about change in a way that you will find more satisfactory and mutually self-developing.

■ Meta-Positive Thinking and TEFCAS

In learning the lessons of Meta-Positive Thinking, you also realize it is essential and invaluable to apply the TEFCAS model when reviewing the way you talk to yourself. In all situations, whether you are being successful, moderately successful, half successful or unsuccessful, Check how you talk to yourself.

Do you use words to deny your Success? When you are successful, do you say things like: 'It was only luck', 'I'll never be able to do that again', 'How embarrassing'? If you do, you are recreating success as a failure and encouraging your brain to change away from the direction of success.

When you fail, do you say things like: 'I quit', 'I can't', 'I never will', 'I told you I'd never succeed', 'I'm useless', 'I'm a failure', I'm hopeless', 'What's the point?', I'll never do that again', 'I give up'?

If you do, you are like a sporting coach who criticizes a five-year-old child. You are focusing on the vulnerable centre of your being; the part that cannot defend itself.

A good way to TEFCAS-check the feedback is to *imagine* yourself as a five-year-old child in whatever you Try, whether it is changing your social skills, changing your business skills, changing your romantic skills, changing your spiritual life or changing your business success. Whatever you do and Try, and whether or not you Succeed, Check what you say to that five-year-old child. If you say 'I've failed', you're pointing your finger at that child, and saying, '*You've* failed'. If you say, 'I'll never succeed', or 'I'll never be able to do that', you're pointing the finger at the child and saying '*You* ... will never succeed'. If you say, 'That was only luck', you're pointing to the child and saying, '*You're* not skilled, or competent, or successful at all, you're just *lucky*.' You're insulting and demeaning the child. In other words, you're insulting and demeaning yourself.

The Positive Change Thinker will look upon him or herself as that five-year-old child and care for it, nurture it and coach it as any ideal coach would: with love, consideration, a constantly positive attitude and unremitting support.

Mastermind

To manage
Change
You must
First
Manage and master
The Manager:

Your Mind

■ Meta-Positive Thinking and Mind Maps

Meta-Positive Thinking is the language the Change Thinker and Change Maker choose to use when interpreting a Mind Map. If you use Meta-Positive principles to interpret your Mind Map you will see with great clarity how to Focus on achieving your ultimate Goal, and what the next steps you need to take will be, in order to progress.

If you find yourself lapsing into Negative Self-Talk you simply need to use Meta-Positive Thinking to focus on your Vision and use TEFCAS to turn your negative reaction into a positive, proactive response.

Before you move on to the next chapter, take another look at the Change Thinking Quotient (CTQ) on page 47. If you redo the questionnaire now, will your score have changed?

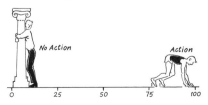

No Action   *Action*

0   25   50   75   100

… the people who are crazy enough to think they can change the world are the ones who do.

Steve Jobs, CEO of Apple

Chapter 8
How change masters change the world

❏ Buzan's Tools for Transformation: 6. Your Change Masters

❏ Choose your Change Masters

❏ Characteristics of Change Masters

❏ You are changing the world

Change Masters are those who have originated great changes in the human condition by their originality of thought and creativity, as well as those who have mastered natural changes and disasters in ways that have benefited great numbers of people. They are commonly known as great geniuses or leaders. As well as the value they add to the general human condition, they can add a special value to your own life. They can become your beacons of positive motivation in times when you are most in need of support. Your Change Masters will act as your mentors, your inspiration and your guides.

During this chapter I am going to introduce you to the characteristics of the Change Masters, to show you how you can develop these strengths in yourself to help you to influence your personal world and manage and embrace change.

■ Your world of change

Just as Aristotle learned from Plato, and Plato from Socrates before him, so the modern Change Thinker will benefit from being aware of previous Change Thinkers and Change Makers and look at what it was that they were trying to understand and manage, thereby reassessing their previous ideas and upgrading previous thoughts with their own. This process leads to progress.

For those who are positive Change Thinkers, the world is full of opportunities to feel hopeful and joyous about the future. There are signs that economic regeneration is bringing new hope to many countries formerly in conflict; that advances in science, technology and medicine are transforming our lives for the better; there is the knowledge that every new generation is born with great levels of energy, enthusiasm and a hunger for discovery; and that the future is an exciting place that we have yet to visit.

At the same time, each of us, at some time in our lives, feels overwhelmed by the nature of the gigantic change that is happening all around us. Many people perceive the current state of the world as depressing. We may feel angry in the wake of the destruction and cruelty of large-scale wars, or powerless in the face of the devastation and starvation created in the wake of plagues and famines. We may be concerned for the future of the earth when we experience the dramatic impact of extreme changes in weather conditions. We may feel fear at the ramifications for society as incidents of crime and vandalism increase, as the economy wavers, or as governments of the day fall short of their promises and potential. At the time of writing, the personal and political impact of violent terrorist attacks is being felt around the world. In the face of these great waves of change it is not unusual to feel helpless and negative.

It is worth remembering that just as the world is in a giant state of flux, so each of us as individuals is intricately interconnected with that flux. You are not without influence. If you change, then the world changes.

Your attitude to change will not only influence your future, it will also affect the lives of friends and family with whom you discuss your ideas – your words and attitude create change in more ways than one.

■ Ripples of change

Think of yourself as a small stone dropped into a calm pond. Each of the ripples created by you, or your action, will radiate out to the edges of the pond – and have an impact beyond where the watery boundary merges with the grassy bank. By your influence, for good or for ill, you will literally have an impact beyond your conscious circle of existence – on friends, on your neighbours, on the air molecules, on the ecosystem, on the outer stratosphere, on the edges of the universe.

Chaos Theory: Scientific theory relating to the irregular and unpredictable behaviour of complex systems that nevertheless have an underlying order.
The Penguin English Dictionary

It is said that the beating of the wing of a butterfly on a small flower in a garden in the countryside of England can trigger a tornado or hurricane that affects Latin America. Many people have humorously misinterpreted this to mean that every butterfly is in the process of causing tornadoes, and therefore that if chaos theory is true the entire world is going to be enveloped shortly in tornadoes that will bring life as we know it to an end! The theory does not mean that every butterfly will cause a tornado. It is confirmation of the fact that everything to some degree affects everything else and that the beating of a butterfly's wing is part of that process.

Put in more immediate, human terms, a conversation, or an email exchange, between two individuals in a small corner of the earth can have ramifications for good or for ill if they choose to join forces and have the belief that they can make a difference.

Therefore the change you make in yourself, if it is a positive change, will feed into the giant flux and flow and will change the probabilities of things happening towards a more positive eventual outcome. The first, best and really *only* way to help bring about personal, business or global change is to bring about a universal change within yourself as you ride the fluxes of time and eternity.

Chaos Butterfly

Tiny Being
Of
Fluttering
Fracturing
Light:

Are you the One?

Are you the Wind-Magician

Whose tiny brushstroke
Wand-stroke
Of Wing-on-air
Has just
Gently
Wing-tapped
Into birth
A Mighty Tornado?

Use this butterfly-centred Mind Map to inspire you to create your own unique picture of transformation moments.

■ Connection through coincidence

How often in life have you been struck by a 'coincidence'? You have flown to California for a major international conference and have taken time out for a quiet lunch. There are thousands of people in attendance and you are not expecting to know anyone. You are irritated when a couple in noisy debate choose to share your table and strike up a conversation. They become interested in the fact that you are British because they have friends in England. It emerges in conversation that they have visited your hometown and you discover that the friends they referred to are in fact former colleagues of yours. How amazing! In fact, the colleagues have spoken about you, in a positive context, because of their respect for your work and the impact it has had on their own. This couple, strangers just moments earlier, are already feeling warm towards you. You don't know them, and they don't know you, but they are interested in your work and are already halfway towards offering friendship and hospitality. You too have adjusted your opinion of them in the light of your respect and liking for your former colleagues, and are no longer bothered by their intrusion. The impact that you have had on your colleagues' lives and they on yours, has had a ripple effect half way around the world. You have a positive feeling about the world and its possibilities.

How different your reaction would have been had you reason to dislike your colleagues. You would have distanced yourself immediately from the couple at the table. You would have felt discomforted by the encounter and would probably have foreshortened your meal. The ripple effect would have been negative – but it would still have had an impact beyond your local boundaries.

■ Creative change

You can become empowered by the knowledge that by changing yourself you can change not only your world, but also the world beyond your shores, and by implication the universe – and indeed you have no choice *but* to change it! You can live the rest of your life confident that your life has value and that your contribution is significant. The more energy you put into your own positive transformation, the more influence you have; if your influence extends to others who also adopt your attitude then you will have made a positive move towards helping to achieve the better world of which most people dream.

You may be thinking: 'I don't want to change the world – I just want my life to be better!' That's fine. Focus on your immediate goal and aim to achieve it in the most positive way possible. Once you have become a Change Maker, the rest will follow.

Imagine what it would be like if *everyone* realized that they were a Change Maker, everyone realized that they *had* to change, everyone loved that realization and everyone realized that they were intimately and intricately interconnected with everyone and everything else in the world and through-out the universe, *and* that by changing themselves positively they would change *everything*. Achieving such a world of change is one of the aims of *Embracing Change*, to help you to reach that kind of realization, to bring about that kind of change in perception, to influence that kind of change in attitude, that kind of change in the world.

■ Live Aid

'Live Aid' was an outdoor concert hosted live on international television via satellite links round the world on 13 July 1985. The previous year, journalist Michael Buerk had produced a news documentary for BBC television, drawing attention to the plight of victims of the famine in Ethiopia. Watching from home, singer/songwriter Bob Geldof was struck by the horror of the situation. Moved to do something about it, he teamed up with a host of popular musicians under the name Band Aid to record a fundraising single. Other countries and organizations followed suit. Early in 1985 the idea of a fundraising concert was suggested and the result mushroomed into sixteen hours of music from around the world, featuring many of the biggest stars of the time, and raising many $1000s. Geldof has said since that the event was bigger than him, that it took on a life of its own – and as testimony to that, the impact continues today.

It went beyond idealism and that ridiculous term activism, which basically means talking about something but doing nothing. We made giving exciting.
Sir Bob Geldof

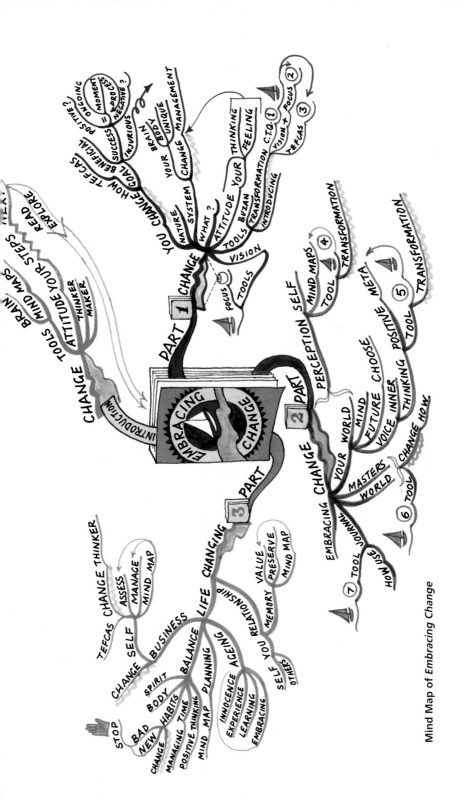

Mind Map of Embracing Change

Mind Map of Buzan's Tools for Transformation

Mind Map of Part I

Mind Map of Part II

Part 2
EMBRACING
CHANGE

Chapter 6 — PERCEPTION
- SELF
- WORLD MIND MAPS
  - EMBRACE / MANAGE / CHOOSE → CHANGE
  - WORLD
- MIND MAPS THINKING RADIANT
  - TOOL
  - WHERE / WHO / HOW SEE → YOU / WORLD / OTHERS
  - WHAT WANT / FUTURE

Chapter 7 — YOUR MIND CHANGING
- FUTURE CHOOSING
- CHANGE VOICE INNER
- POSITIVE THINKING
  - POSITIVE
  - NEGATIVE
  - META STEPS
  - TOOL

Chapter 9 — JOURNAL CHANGE
- PLAN LIFE
- TOOL
- MIND MAPS = MASTERS CHANGE
  - SEQUENCE
  - HOW USE
  - BENEFITS
  - TEFCAS
  - FOCUS
  - VISION
  - META POSITIVE THINKING

Chapter 8 — MASTERS CHANGE
- YOU
- WORLD
- CHOOSE
  - PERSONAL
  - HISTORIC
- CHARACTERISTICS ENERGY ORIENTED GOAL
  - COMMITMENT
  - DESIRE
  - COURAGE
  - PERSISTENCE
  - ENTHUSIASM
  - ATTITUDE POSITIVE
  - LOVE TASK
- FLEXIBILITY BELIEF SELF
  - INTUITION
  - LEARNING
  - MENTAL LITERACY
  - TRUTH
  - SUBJECT KNOWLEDGE

Mind Map of Part III

Mind Map of the Mind Maps you can create to make your Change Vision

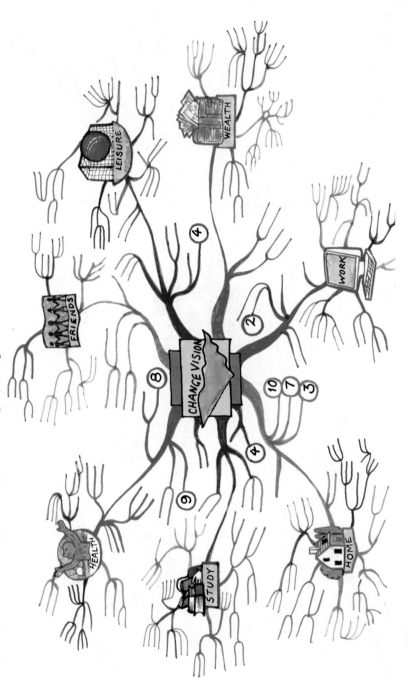

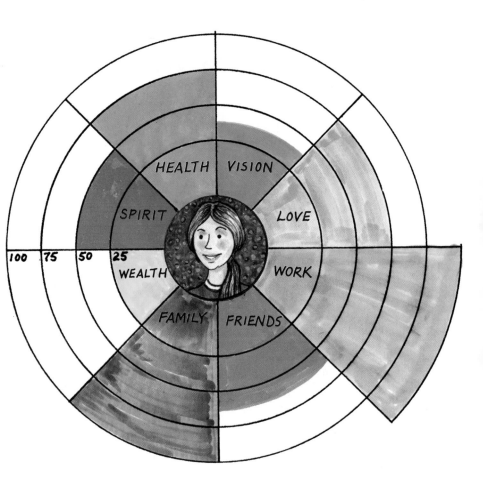

An example of the Change Wheel

Joy's story

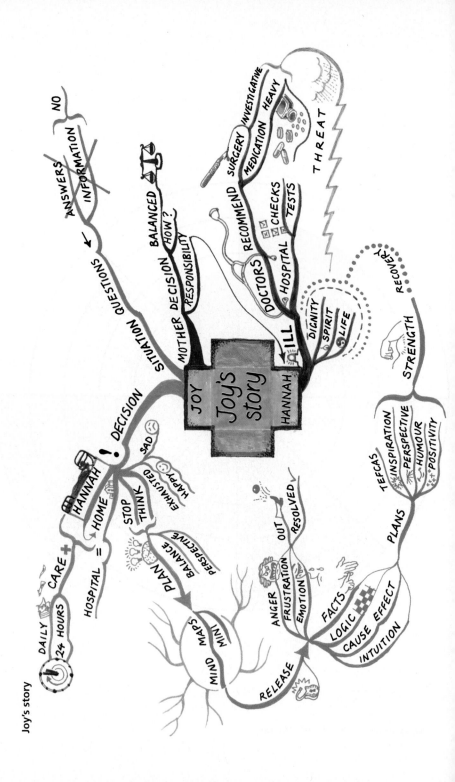

◼ Who are your Change Masters?

To face the challenges of self-management and achieving our goals, we each need the help of mentors and role models. Whether you are choosing to bring about a significant change in your life, or whether you are being forced to face a change, you will need about you a support group of people who can encourage, guide and influence you in a positive way to make the transition the most positive, edifying and life-expanding period possible.

You may be fortunate enough to be surrounded by such people already; or you may be feeling very much alone with your vision of the future. Either way, I would encourage you to open your mind to the fact that there are millions of people out there who are ready to help you. Some you will be acquainted with, some you will not have met yet. Others may have departed this earth for decades – but their influence lives on, and they can be a major source of inspiration and direction. No, I am not talking about communing with the dead, I am talking about reading and learning – about influential Change Thinkers and Change Makers who have faced the future with tenacity.

I am going to introduce you to a 'baker's dozen' of these Change Masters from which you can select your own personal favourites. But first, think about those who influence you now.

◼ Choose your Change Masters

Take a moment to think about who you have as your own personal support network of Change Thinkers. If you are about to make an important decision, if you have just had a piece of catastrophic news that will change the course of your life, who do you turn to for solace or advice? It will be different people in different circumstances: perhaps a long-standing and trusted friend in the case of a relationship break-up; perhaps a parent or sibling in the case of a close bereavement; perhaps your former boss if you are facing redundancy, or your doctor if you have discovered an unplanned pregnancy.

Take a large piece of blank paper, and write down all those people who comprise your support network in different areas of your life. This will be of most benefit to you if done in Mind Map format (see Chapter 6).

⬧ Characteristic	Buzan's Tools for Transformation
1. Goal-orientated	Your FOCUS on achieving the end result.
2. Self-belief	Your CTQ – indicating Faith in yourself and in the universe.
3. Desire	Your VISION – driving the passion and motivation to succeed.
4. Commitment	Total dedication to achieving your VISION.
5. Creativity	Imagination and Radiant Thinking released via MIND MAPS.
6. Planning	Powerfully summarized by MIND MAPS.
7. Risk-taking/ Intuition	The TRY in TEFCAS that is needed before any chance of SUCCESS.
8. Persistence	The TRY and TRY again in TEFCAS.
9. Subject knowledge	Gaining experience through TEFCAS EVENTS, through MIND MAPS, and from the FEEDBACK and counsel of CHANGE MASTERS.
10. Learning	Often through mistakes: this is the CHECK and ADJUST provided by TEFCAS and MIND MAPS.
11. Mental literacy	Awareness of how the BRAIN works and enhancing its function through the use of BUZAN'S TOOLS.
12. Enthusiasm	The result of the SUCCESS in TEFCAS and the manifestation of META-POSITIVE THINKING.
13. Positive attitude	Encapsulated by META-POSITIVE THINKING.
14. Love of the task	Those who love what they do are constantly joyful as a result of META-POSITIVE THINKING.
15. Truth	Clarity and honesty is provided via the VISION of MIND MAPS and the FEEDBACK in TEFCAS.
16. Courage	Pure META-POSITIVE THINKING combined with FOCUS.
17. Flexibility	Creative flexibility and speed of thought are the result of using MIND MAPS and TEFCAS to transform your ideas.

18. Energy	This is your true wealth: your Mental, Physical and Spiritual balance, to be safeguarded and nurtured by using all the change TOOLS appropriately.
19. Change Masters: Historic	These are iconic figures who can offer inspiration through their personal attributes and their achievements. They are perfect exponents of the Tools for Transformation.
20. Change Masters: Personal	These precious people are your personal support group and mentors who will be truthful and who will be constructively supportive of your ambitions in bringing about personal change.

See the following pages for an explanation of the power of these characteristics and how, when consciously applied, they can transform their equal and opposite negative forms.

■ The importance of non-conformity

One of the most interesting characteristics of our Change Masters is a common tendency to be non-conformist. Change implies doing something that is different to the norm – so whether it is outside the norm of your own usual behaviour, or outside the norm of society or the norm of accepted thought, there is an implication that 'the rules' may need to be modified. A positive Change Thinker understands and facilitates this. I am not recommending anarchic self-interest here. I am recommending an awareness that, because something has 'always' been done in a particular way, it does not mean that it is either right, or a requirement, to continue to do it or look at it in the same way.

Rules are implemented literally as a measure to manage change but, as we have already seen, change is its own manager. Fixed rules or habits that are never reviewed can over time become disastrously inappropriate. A Change Thinker will realize when the time has arrived for the rules to be updated in order to deal with a new situation of change. Changes are likely to be resisted by those who have become reliant upon the rules for their own sake, as a 'safety blanket' of stability that makes sense of their immediate world, but 'breaking the rules' in given instances is not only a Good Idea, it is necessary for survival. A creative Change Thinker will recognize this and be ready to make the new rules. This is again an ongoing process and is an example of thinking with renewed Innocence in the light of Experience (see page 262).

In order to bring about change you need to have the courage of your convictions. No-one is suggesting that this is an easy process; that is why drawing on the experience and expertise of those Change Masters with knowledge and experience who have gone before you is an invaluable and essential part of your Change 'repertoire'.

■ Thirteen Change Masters

Thirteen Change Masters make a baker's dozen. You see – even the baker who first challenged the rules has gone down in history!

The following Change Masters are a representative sample of many hundreds of extraordinary men and women throughout history who, from varied backgrounds, and in different ways, have brought about positive change in our society. They are inspirational figures who have lent wisdom and guidance to my own aspirations and actions.

The Change Masters share the twenty characteristics listed above, which show them to be Change Thinkers and Change Makers, dynamic and flexible in approach, courageous and tenacious in attitude; intellectuals or creative thinkers who were not afraid to face their fears and take a stand for their beliefs.

The advantage of referring to historical figures is that they are far enough removed from the present day to have become icons in their fields – and in that regard are robust in their reputation and fairly unshakeable as reliable virtual mentors. At the same time, their personal challenges and characteristics will have resonance with the issues and events we face today.

You will have your own favourites who you may want to use instead – but these are my particular mentors, who in various and multiple ways have overcome all kinds of obstacles in the pursuit of their goals.

Philosophy and Logic: Aristotle (384–322BC)

Aristotle's own Change Master was Plato. He passed on Plato's legacy of thought to Alexander the Great, whom he tutored for seven years. Aristotle's theories of logic and reason brought about a renaissance of thought and intellectual endeavour. His search for facts and his invention of a codification system make him a champion of TEFCAS and the need for Truth.

He is the perfect Change Master for all those who need to look at the facts in order to keep their feet firmly on the ground. Mind Maps are the perfect tool for achieving this.

Mathematics: Archimedes (287–212BC)

Archimedes was influenced by his father, Pheidias, who was an astronomer. His imaginative inventions and the results of his mathematical research changed our perception of the universe forever. His early Sand Reckoner was a device to measure the dimensions of the universe. His later findings included the water-displacement theory. He had a highly organized and intelligent mind and was greatly influenced by his teacher, Euclid. He was also a directed daydreamer, which enhanced his creative imagination and his ability as a Change Thinker of genius.

He is a Change Master who offers inspiration for all those whose Vision takes them into the realm of the unknown, and is a reminder of the importance of your Change Thinker group.

Strategic thought: Sun Tzu (c.300BC)

At the time Alexander the Great was advancing towards the east with his army of Macedonians, Greeks and Persians, a Chinese general and thinker, Sun Tzu, was expounding his own philosophy of war, based upon the Taoist search for balance and harmony. Sun Tzu is a champion of victory through intelligence – by 'knowing your enemy' – in war and in peace.

As a Change Master he is an inspirational example of the benefits of Planning and Non-conformity – being flexible in thought and original in action.

Communication: Alexander Graham Bell (1847–1922)

The mobile phone revolution has at its root a man whose prime motivation was to find a way for deaf people to communicate more effectively. The inventor of the telephone, Alexander Graham Bell, was greatly influenced by his father, Alexander Melville Bell, elocutionist and the inventor of 'visible speech' by which deaf people were taught to speak by understanding the appropriate position of the vocal chords. The younger Alexander became greatly concerned with the needs of those suffering from deafness and it was this that motivated him to begin experimenting with acoustic devices. He founded the Bell Telephone Company when the Western Union Telegraph Company rejected the offer to buy his patent.

He is a Change Master who represents benevolence in that his goal was not monetary wealth but healthy balance for others.

Science and Astronomy: Copernicus (1473–1543)

Known as the founder of modern astronomy, Copernicus was widely travelled and hungry to increase his learning. The first to demonstrate that the Earth is not the centre of the universe, he literally changed the way we view our world. Even now when we say the sun is rising, we mean that the earth is spinning. It is hard to overcome the evidence of our eyes.

He is a Change Master who represents Courage and Risk-Taking in that his views were at the time in radical opposition to those of the Church and he risked severe punishment in apparently denying the core of religious belief.

Arts: William Blake (1757–1827)

Poet, painter, engraver and visionary, Blake was a radical spirit fired by genius; a fabulous revolutionary who was constantly talking about change. Embracing change as a route to finding paradise is at the root of his work. 'In the visionary imagination of William Blake there is no birth and no death, no beginning and no end, only the perpetual pilgrimage within time towards eternity.' So says Peter Ackroyd in his biography *Blake* (1995).

As a Change Master he represents Creativity and the Imagination and the concept that all things are connected.

Natural History: Charles Darwin (1809–82)

Darwin is noted in history as the person who discovered the theory of evolution by natural selection. He recognized that the species of the world need to change constantly in order to survive. His part, as a naturalist, in a five-year mission of scientific discovery on *HMS Beagle* has inspired generations of scientists and explorers. His revolutionary conclusion, that human beings are primates, still remains the forefront of religious debate today. Darwin represents Persistence, Truth and Knowledge.

Politics: Abraham Lincoln (1809–65)

This radical and courageous politician oversaw the unification of the nation following the devastation of the Civil War in America and changed the law of the land to abolish slavery. He was a champion of equality and a superb orator whose skills of communication eventually won the nation over to peace. Assassinated by John Wilkes Booth on 14 April 1865, Lincoln is remembered as a fair and direct man who was 'steadfast in principle' and of strict morality.

As a Change Master he is an inspirational example of someone driven by a desire for positive change, who has an incisive intelligence, commitment and flexibility in abundance and who was firmly focused on achieving his Goal. He is also a powerful example of TEFCAS in action as he 'failed' in many of his attempts to gain the presidency – but kept on Trying until he succeeded.

Business: Andrew Carnegie (1835–1918)

Andrew Carnegie, industrialist and custodian of wealth, is an excellent example of a Change Maker. By far the richest man in the world, he amassed great wealth via the oil and steel industries. When he reached the zenith of his commercial success, his philanthropic drive led him to invest extensively in educational resources. He still ranks as the greatest contributor in the last 1,000 years to libraries, museums and the arts and sciences.

As a Change Master he is a fine example of Vision and Focus, and Risk-taking. His positive attitude fed his success and his commitment to his goal led him to attain financial wealth and a generosity of spirit.

Engineering/technology: Isambard Kingdom Brunel (1806–59)

A brilliant engineer from a difficult background whose vision changed the landscape of transport systems and communication networks around the world. He is a wonderful example because he came from a disadvantaged background but during his lifetime used his imagination and his genius to change the landscape of the planet – absolutely extraordinary. He changed the landscape, changed design, changed transportation, changed people's ideas, changed the future of the world. In 2000 he was voted by UK TV viewers the Second Greatest Briton of the millennium.

As a Change Master he is an inspiration; an example of what a visionary can do if he or she makes plans and consciously learns from mistakes as he or she progresses.

Social transformation: Mohandas K (Mahatma) Gandhi (1869–1948)

Mahatma (the name means Great Soul) Gandhi showed that freedom for India could be achieved without resorting to violence. He challenged British rule and championed a movement of non-violent resistance that inspired the world. He changed the future of his country and had a permanent impact on world attitudes to peaceful protest.

As a Change Master, Gandhi represents hopefulness and faith, combined with logical thought. His methods were a physical manifestation of the Mind Map approach to change.

Education: Maria Montessori (1870–1952)

Many of my books use Maria Montessori as an example because she is such an exciting example of someone who is willing to break with tradition in order to achieve a positive goal. Her radical influence transformed the ways in which the world thought about educating young children and their ability to change. Her work with handicapped children led her to appreciate how the young mind is stimulated by shape, colour and texture. She abandoned rigid forms of teaching and instead encouraged freedom of expression and emphasized the importance of self-discipline. Her influence is expanding even further today.

As a Change Master she represents Vision, Creativity, Joyfulness and Commitment. Her intuitive approach demonstrated great intelligence, and her methodology – in recognizing the importance of sound, shape, texture and colour in stimulating the minds of children during the learning process – is manifest at the very heart of Mind Maps.

Competition: Morihei Ueshiba (1883–1969)

The father of Aikido, O Sensei was arguably history's greatest martial artist. Even in his eighties he could disarm any foe. Although invincible as a warrior (he served as an infantryman in the Russo-Japanese War), he was above all a man of peace who detested violence. 'The Way of the Warrior has been misunderstood as a means to kill and destroy others. Those who seek competition are making a grave mistake. To smash, injure or destroy is the worst sin a human being can commit. The real Way of a Warrior is to prevent slaughter – it is the Art of Peace, the power of Love.'

As a Change Master he is a valuable role model and a striking example of the value of Truth.

■ How Change Masters transform Change Thinking

It is at times when we are feeling totally overwhelmed and believe that all things are hopeless, or at times when we are looking for inspiration to reach that ultimate goal, that our Change Masters can be of most benefit. Our 'internal' Change Masters will provide example and inspiration. Our 'external' Change Masters can provide more emotional and practical help and feedback. These will include friends and family, and many and increasing numbers of organizations and charities that are specifically focused on helping you to bring about a positive transformation when you are at a nadir in your life – in other words, to help you to manage change.

Under pressure we are very likely to be tempted to retreat into negative thinking. The inspiration and example of our Change Master Group can help us to 'see off' the trappings of negative attitudes that hold us back, and prevent us from fulfilling our true potential.

By 'negative' I mean that these are factors and influences that inhibit change progressing *in the direction* that you want it. They are actually generating just as much change as the positive, proactive response, it's just that the avoidance tactic obliges you and encourages you to change in a negative direction; or worse, to change by attempting to resist changing, and therefore regressing.

Returning to our earlier metaphor, if you decide to try not to change, rather than stay static you become like a person who stops swimming midstream. You will be carried away, farther and farther from your goal. You are likely to change from being a free agent to feeling fearful, self-imprisoned, and to regard yourself as a 'failure'.

■ The surf rider revisited

The one thing you can rely on is that everything will change, that change will take place at very different rhythms, speeds and accelerations, and a lot of change is quite slow and gentle. You can learn to ride those waves of change, because, to return to our ocean metaphor, you know that the ocean is constantly changing.

If you can predict the rhythms of the change then you can ride them to your advantage. So the fact that all is constantly changing gives you your strength, gives you your foundation, gives you your base, gives you your confidence, and takes away the stress, because you suddenly realize there are patterns to much constant change.

When you come to understand that change *will* happen, you can 'get the big picture', monitor it, and move on. Being strong when a sudden change 'out of nowhere comes' will enable you to become far more adaptable and flexible because you are already a confident surf rider. If there is a sudden blip – as if the rhythm of the wave changed suddenly – and you fall off your surfboard, you will be able to recover far more quickly because you will have become a far better surf rider, much more able to get back up.

The top surf riders have phenomenal skill derived from accumulated knowledge and experience. When they make a mistake, when they mis-estimate the rhythm of the change, they are immediately able to get back up and take the next one *because of their knowledge of the constancy of certain aspects of change.*

To look at this from a different perspective: the constancy of change and the constancy of certain rhythms of change offers you security in another way as well, in that you come to realize that to bring about change, to ride certain rhythms, you need to predict them and to take them one wave at a time; one step at a time.

When we combine the power and impact of our own thoughts in a way that is congruent with those Change Thinkers and Change Makers who have overcome immense adversity to achieve greatness, we combine our brain capacity with theirs, and increase our potential to achieve success to an infinite degree.

■ An armoury of change tactics

The following characteristics are common human responses to change. Using the inspiration and experience provided by your Change Master Group I will show you how negative characteristics can be turned into naturally positive ones; each meta-negative response can be countered by a Change Thinker Characteristic.

'I CAN'T BECAUSE ...

... I'm Scared'

It is normal to be fearful when faced with change. The process of change is often accompanied by a period of disruption and acute discomfort and therefore there is reluctance for people to embrace it fully. They don't want to embrace their new emerging reality because it means letting go of their old familiar reality; this is true no matter how uncomfortable they are. They are afraid of the change because it often appears as chaos, and the future is an unknown and uncertain prospect.

The person who recognizes himself (or herself) to be an agent of change, will realize that he is taking part in an ongoing process and will understand that to progress as an individual, to realize fully the changes that are happening, he will need to integrate the change. He will need to apply TEFCAS (see pages 72–85). In order to assimilate the new characteristics, he will need to stay with it for a while, adjust to the new relative norm and then move on to the next developmental stage.

As described in the earlier chapters, we have to keep moving, keep changing, in order to remain as we are; but at the same time we have the capacity to bring about profound change – provided we go 'with' the process, trust the universe and sit with, and assimilate, our ever-changing state. This is not the same as being fatalistic or complacent, far from it. This is a process of active engagement with the change as it occurs.

If you look your fear in the face, and sit with it for a while until it is familiar, you can transform it into its equal and opposite: COURAGE. Courage does not mean the absence of fear; courage is the state of looking fear in the face and having the faith and the belief in the change process to see it through.

Change Maker Characteristic: Courage

Courage comes into the scene when you feel that somehow you are endangering yourself, by taking a particular path in handling change. Many people in life who are labelled as courageous following an extraordinary act, dismiss the term and say they were 'only doing their job', that they were 'acting instinctively'. These are people who were so much 'in the moment' that they drew on their intuitive experience, took stock fast and acted instinctively, in a Super-Intelligent manner. They are true Change Makers, who recognize that Risk is an inevitable and integral part of life. They have recognized in a cataclysmic moment that it is more dangerous NOT to change than to risk everything.

Avoiding danger is no safer in the long run than outright exposure.
Life is either a daring adventure or nothing
Helen Keller

Once you realize that a state of change is the constant, and that all is flux, then, on one level, acting rather than resisting ceases to require courage. Our responses as adults are not so very far removed from playing in the playground. Remember those early risks, when you jumped off a climbing frame, did your first somersault, or risked rejection by approaching and speaking to a new 'friend'? We never lose that state of play – provided we don't close ourselves off from it.

There is an *apparent* contradiction within everything being in flux, because if everything is in flux then there is a constant. Therefore everything *isn't* in flux, although *everything* is *always* in flux. This is a nice concept to play around with, but it becomes rather like getting stuck in a little whirlpool! You stop the whirlpool by realizing that the Truth is that in all this change, there is a constant, and the constant is that everything will keep on changing. That is the secure base from which you can examine the flow in the flux and the change.

'... I've Just Got To Do This First'

Procrastination means not bringing about the change you desire, by constantly escaping into *excuse pathways* in order to avoid doing what it is you are supposed to do. However, by avoiding the change that you want, you are changing anyway, and you are changing towards the probability that the change you want will not happen.

Procrastination is a decision to change *away* from the goal you desire.

We procrastinate for a number of reasons, not through any lack of will or lack of knowledge but simply because the vision that we have created for ourselves is not clear or compelling enough to oblige us to continue towards it. It can be related to fear of success – in which the fear of the results of the change brings about the change towards non-change – one of the most dangerous syndromes in which the brain can become involved.

If you know that you procrastinate, be aware that procrastination can camouflage itself very neatly in a variety of cunning ways. It loves domestic chores: cooking, cleaning, shopping, letter writing – all the tasks you normally avoid become your main priorities. It is philanthropic. It loves doing favours for others, and will convince you that your neighbour/ son/ friend – even your worst enemy – cannot survive a moment longer unless you offer or agree to help them in some way.

But to see it as separate from you is of course to feed the worst aspect of procrastination. It may feel as if there is someone else's voice inside your head telling you what to do, but in fact you are just avoiding responsibility. You are the Manager of your Mind. So, to beat procrastination keep your Plan in mind at all times. Commit your goals and priorities to paper. If you find yourself at such an impasse, use Mind Maps (see Chapter 6) to refocus your vision and to prioritize your next actions. Mind Mapping is a powerful tool to move from Change Thinking to Change Making. Use TEFCAS to monitor your progress, one step at a time, and you will see that the ultimate goal is both identifiable and achievable.

The next time the voice in your head offers you a distraction from the task in hand, remember you are your own inner coach. You are talking to yourself.

Change Maker Characteristic: Vision and Focus

To overcome both Procrastination and Complacency you need to refocus, as described in Buzan's Second Tool For Transformation in Chapter 4. Focus is enlightening and encourages you to take action. Focus allows you to adapt to the opportunities the world gives you and to be aware of your ability to forge your own path energetically, delightedly, enthusiastically, and direct yourself towards your chosen goal.

'…I Won't Be Good Enough'

Procrastination can be related to perfectionism – in that the fear of producing something that is less than ideal can prevent us from taking the first step towards achievement.

However, this attitude assumes that perfection cannot be achieved (which is a negative thought); I am saying something profoundly different – that perfection can *always* be achieved provided that you have done the very best that you can in that moment. There is the potential for perfection in each state of your TEFCAS journey, onward to your ultimate goal.

■ Grown to perfection

I was once told a story by a First Nation American Indian Chief who had become a modern American super-executive in a computer company. He had spent a lot of time with disadvantaged kids on the reservations, many of whom had been abused on all levels. They were very depressed about who they were and believed they could never achieve anything in life.

He would take them to a weed patch or flowerbed and show them the flowers. He would show them the dandelions, and the roses, and ask: 'Which one of these flowers is not a flower? Which one of these flowers is not a *beautiful* flower? Which one of these beautiful flowers is not *perfect*? *You*, my children, are just the same as the flowers. *You* are beautiful; *you* are perfect.'

I would add that you can *choose* whether to pick off your own petals; you can *choose* whether to water (nurture) yourself; you can *choose* whether to damage or destroy other flowers – but at the moment, you are a flower, and you are perfect as you are right now. You decide what happens to the flower.

Your destination – the ultimate perfection – is important, but if you are going along the path in the right way, you become like a child. Would you look at a child and say he or she was not perfect? Each child is perfect in its own right, and each human is perfect in their own right at that moment. Whatever they are is precisely what they are at that moment, and they're in the process of change. The goal, their ultimate vision, leads them towards an improvement, step by step in their development. Their achievement at each stage can be considered to be perfect.

By the very nature of change, once you have achieved your aim, in order to maintain the momentum of your success, you will be seeking ever greater heights. Your current target is a stepping stone, a single moment in the pathway of your life.

'... I Can't Be Bothered'

Complacency is a close relation of procrastination and is tantamount to non-action. It's the equivalent of floating on your back in a stream, and saying that you don't care and it doesn't matter where the stream is flowing.

Complacency is the active consideration not to act

Complacency leads you into being taken wherever the current takes you; you become completely irresponsible for your actions, you become the object of all the forces acting upon you rather than being the subject driving those forces. Complacency implies non-action, non-direction, non-change, but this is a trap.

If you are complacent you change anyway, but you drift towards negative change.

Living life with no plan, with no concept of where you are headed, leads inevitably to 'non-arrival' at any preconceived destination. Perpetual drift means that you will be forced always to adapt to survive whatever life throws at you. This is not necessarily a problem; many thousands live their lives this way, but you are never going to achieve your full potential, because you are not taking full responsibility for living your life proactively. You are more likely to feel like a victim of fate than a Change Thinker with freedom of choice.

Actors' Conundrum

| When I Choose, I act. | When I Choose Not To Act, I Act. | Therefore I have No choice But to be An Actor. | All the World's My Stage ... |

Many great thinkers and change makers have said things such as ' It is the journey that is important, not the destination' or 'Focus on the pathway rather than the goal' or 'We should focus on the means rather than the ends'. These quite sensible statements are often misinterpreted by those who do not understand the nature of change. These statements are intended to be, and are in fact, inclusive. If you focus only on the *means* to achievement, and don't have a goal, you will behave like a wind-up toy that scampers off in all directions – shooting around at random and rapidly winding down to a halt, having fundamentally gone nowhere. If you focus only on the change *goal*, you will be extremely inefficient in accomplishing that goal, because the means by which you achieve it will not be the most appropriate.

What you, the Change Thinker, have to do is to ensure that you hold your goal constantly in mind as a beacon, while simultaneously concentrating on the best method of achieving that Change Goal.

To better understand the course of the Journey and the means whereby you complete the Journey, look again at the Feedback, Check, Adjust sections of TEFCAS. To review your Vision, focus on Success, the next Trial and the Event from that Trial.

Change Maker Characteristic: Commitment

Commitment occurs when, having refined your vision, having the desire to achieve it, to bring about the change, having the belief in yourself that you can do that, you dedicate yourself to it.

To bring about that degree of change, it is powerful to commit to both writing it down and vocalizing it to others. Writing down externalizes it for you and gives you a kind of feedback; it increases the probability that your vision will become a reality. Vocalizing to other people is helpful because in a sense you have put yourself 'on the line'. Once you've voiced your commitment to others, if you have a good Change Master group, they will help you remain true to the task, to have faith and to be committed.

'... I Feel So Helpless'

Feelings of helplessness stem from being overwhelmed by something over which you feel you have no direct control. Each person's life has its own unique set of challenges and we often feel at our most inadequate when we are watching someone we care about go through a difficult period of change. It can be the hardest thing in the world to view another's pain and not be able to so something practical to appease their anguish.

You cannot live another's life. No matter how much you would like to, you cannot take the burden of change *away* from them. You can however 'be there' for them and, by listening and contributing, enable them to transform the change into something that is beneficial in some way.

Helplessness itself is a process of change. It leads into a negatively synergetic spiral of depression. When you feel you're help-LESS, your vitality (life force) is reduced, your optimism and hopefulness decline, your posture slouches, your breathing becomes more shallow, your senses more dull, and the internal processes of all your circulatory and glandular systems become more sluggish. You change – to your disadvantage. If you change to your disadvantage, then you also change to everybody else's, to the world's and to the universe's disadvantage.

You are not help-LESS, you are help-FULL

The minute that you realize that you are in no way help-LESS, you become help-FULL. Every second of your life can be devoted to both thinking and acting in a positive way, to managing change as change, if it were a living being, would wish to be managed.

Change Maker Characteristic: Hopefulness

Hopefulness represents the whole of meta-positive thinking. Hopefulness means having a vision, believing you can achieve it, and having access to the methodology by which you can get to it. Real hopefulness is not wishful thinking, it is the thought of the goal combined with the knowledge of the processes of how to get there, and the fact that you are capable of engaging in those processes. Literally it means 'full of hope'.

■ The Samaritans

This international charity founded by Chad Varah is made up of a veritable 'army' of volunteers from all walks of life who provide a 24-hour listening service for those who are depressed, in despair and who have suicidal feelings. They are not an advice agency; they cannot 'cure' people's problems, nor can they, ultimately, prevent someone from taking their own life if they are intent on doing so. Yet hundreds of thousands of people call every day to speak to an anonymous, constructive listener, who cares.

The listeners help each caller to see 'the bigger picture', to draw back from the edge of despair and to face another day – to become hope-FULL. This is TEFCAS in action, as each small step leads towards positive change.

'... I Don't Want To Do It On My Own'

Loneliness is a state of mind. You can be lonely in a crowd, or content on your own up a mountain. Feelings of loneliness are linked to your sense of self-esteem and self-worth. In fact, you are never alone. In your internal universe every one of the habit patterns in your brain can be considered like a separate individual. So you are not a single individual, you are a planet's worth of individuals.

The capacity of your brain to create patterns of thought, i.e. negative habits or positive habits, is '1' followed by ten and a half million kilometres of typewritten noughts! That's how big your private support network is. You have as many friends in your head as you need. If you find yourself in an environment that you feel is personally threatening in some way, increase the band and the strength of your internal friends. Fantasy friends are a resource that children use quite naturally all the time.

In your external universe you can take stock afresh of those you know, and consider those you have not yet met. There are like-minded change-thinking souls in this world who can nourish and support you, to help you achieve your goals. If you feel you haven't met them yet, ask yourself why, and what you need to do to change your environment, your social pattern, your leisure habits, in order to meet them. Use your Mind Map Journal to explore this further and begin to change your social world.

Change Maker Characteristic: Enthusiasm

Enthusiasm: A noun *meaning* possession by a god, inspiration, intense interest, passion, excitement, zeal, fervour. When I found out the root of this word, it became highly significant and much more meaningful than I had previously realized. The essence of enthusiasm is the central *thus* which comes from the Greek *theos*, meaning God. When you are en-*thus*-iastic therefore, it means that you are manifesting the energy of God or the Universe. This is a considerable degree of energy with which to help you to bring about change! It is an energy that cannot help but draw others to you. You are therefore gifted with the capability of bringing about change in yourself and helping others bring about change in themselves. This helps explain why martial arts Change Master Morihei Ueshiba and other great spiritual leaders referred to either the energy of the Universe or the energy of God flowing through you.

'…I Feel So Depressed'

Loneliness is often linked to Depression. When you feel depressed you retreat into your body. Depression literally means that. De-pressed. Everything is depressed, pressed down. Your motivation is down, your posture is down, your energy levels are down, sensory systems, down, breathing efficiency, down, everything, down, down, down. The way out of this is to make maximum use of your Change Thinker support network – whether made up of Change Makers that you see every day, or 'Super' Change Makers of iconic status. Combine this with conscious Meta-Positive Thinking and if you link this to your Vision of the future – you *will* change in a positive direction.

Change Maker Characteristic: Laughter

Laughter is pure positive energy – provided it is directed in a positive manner. Laughter is the brain's joyous reaction to a sudden delicious change in perception, a mini paradigm shift in an awareness of the relationships between things.

The pun is often derided as being the lowest form of wit: however, the pun is the *highest* form of wit, it is the twisting of metaphors. Aristotle said that metaphor is the highest form of thinking; and the greatest punster in the history of the English language was one William Shakespeare. You will find my own little ditty on puns overleaf.

The pun's 'the lowest form of wit'
To those who cannot master it.

Laughter is an ecstatic response that occurs when the brain lights up at the realization of the interrelationship between things. Laughter is orgasmic in its effect, giving you a complete physical workout. The physical actions of laughter take you through aerobic exercise, flexible and strengthening exercise, and at the same time encourage you to breathe – to exhale and inhale deeply – which enlivens your senses, and gives your muscles – especially those of your diaphragm and your back, arms, face, chest and stomach – a comprehensive workout. Every single one of the muscles is involved in a rhythmical response, so it is also like a giant massage.

Laughter reduces stress and tension, and makes you more attractive to be with; which is another reason why a Change Agent should make sure that they are either laughing themselves or are in social situations where they laugh. Successful and happy people are fun to be with; they add energy, fuel and impetus to the changes they are bringing about.

'... It Will Never Work'

Cynicism is a manipulative form of proudly negative thinking that ensures that the cynic is always right. The cynic will protect him or herself in a false cloak of accuracy, pointing out negative things that are true but not dominantly true, basking in the correct assumption that things will *always* go badly because their attitude and their actions combine to ensure that they *do* go badly. The cynic is the person who points out that people *always* make mistakes, and he or she is right – because 1 per cent or 10 per cent or 20 per cent of the time people *do* make mistakes. This is a positive thing because the more each person tries, the more mistakes he or she will make – and the closer they will be to achieving their goals. The cynic does not view life this way. The cynic, voicing a negative prediction about his or her own future, tends to be 100 per cent correct because they make it so, and they can then confirm how clever they are by saying, 'I told you so.'

The cynic is often too afraid to Try for Success

If you find yourself voicing cynical thoughts, check your inner coach and adjust your self-talk. Apply TEFCAS to your everyday activities and pay particular attention to how you Check the Feedback and Adjust your behaviour. The more honest you can be about your true goals, the more likely you are to achieve them.

Change Maker Characteristic: Risk-taking

Those who try to bring about change are taking risks. Because they are taking risks, they have the inevitable probability of having learning experiences along the way that they weren't expecting. Therefore they may not, on a percentage basis, be as successful as those who do not Try as often, but they are infinitely more successful in terms of bringing about positive change, because they are the only ones who are *doing* it. So you may say that the positive thinker is infinitely more capable, the enthusiast infinitely more capable, of bringing about positive change, because the cynic will bring about *no* positive change. **Special note:** This is not the same as becoming a dare-devil or a change addict. See pages 201–202.

' ... I'll Never Change'

In extreme, the knowledge that you can *never* change leads to addictive behaviour. Your belief is that your behaviour is directed from outside yourself, that you are in some way 'weak-willed' and that you have no control over your thoughts or desires. This is far from the truth. Your brain is very much in control – but is in the grip of a Big Bad Habit. When you develop addictive thoughts or compulsive behaviour, your brain becomes trapped in Meta-*Negative* Thinking, which is like a huge black hole that draws all your activity towards it. You therefore continue to change at an accelerating rate into an area that you may wish to avoid or that is damaging to you.

> *Whether you think you can, or think you can't – you're right.*
> **Henry Ford**

The way to change this behaviour is consciously to apply Meta-*Positive* Thinking – making sure that you coach your Inner Change voice to talk to you in a very positive way (see page 113–15) and to remember that Persistence is your key to ongoing Success.

■ Escape from the black hole of addiction

The immediate effect of applying Meta-Positive Thinking is to put your Spaceship, which is being drawn into a black hole, into Warp Drive Level 1. This will not be enough to get you out of the hole immediately; however, the constant repetition of the Meta-Positive Thinking habit/ affirmation/ phrase will increase your Warp Drive to Level 2. The more you increase your Meta-Positive Thinking the more Warp Drive power you add to your ship, until you reach the critical Warp Drive Level which will draw you **away** from the black hole and your addictive behaviour towards a Meta-Positive Thinking Habit.

Change Master Characteristic: Persistence

In bringing about any change or transformation the engine of that change is your persistence. Persistence is your T in TEFCAS. It is, if you like, the starter engine or the key in the starter engine: the continued application of that engine to the bringing about of change. The minute you stop Trying, the minute you stop persisting, then change continues without you being a conscious part of it.

Persistence is the energy that drives you toward your Vision; it is strongly associated with your willpower. The closer you come to your Goal the more the gravitational force of that Goal, like a giant star, will draw you towards it and the more energy your persistence will generate. Persistence is like the rocket fuel that propels your spaceship towards a star.

It is worth noting that many great Change Masters have said that persistence is the key to their success. Many achievements have resulted when those who have Tried and Tried and Tried, and have been on the verge of giving up, have taken the decision to Try 'just one more time'. It is that 'one more time' that brings about great change. It is Persistence that leads to the great Successes.

■ O Sensei's metaphor of the wellspring

Morihei Ueshiba, 'O Sensei', the founder of Aikido, stated that maintaining the direction of your energy toward keeping your dream alive is simply a matter of allowing it to continue to *flow*. It does not have to be a great rush of energy. He used the metaphor of a tiny wellspring underneath a polluted pool. If that tiny stream continues to flow without pause or hesitation, then it will cleanse the pool, constantly, and the pollution of the pool will never enter that jet of pure, clear water.

In the context of change, this means that constant, positive, directed energy has great value regardless of the environment. This energy is encapsulated in the character traits of Commitment and Persistence. These are two of the major qualities of the Change Thinker.

'… I Can't Afford To'

This common cry is often used to explain why action is impossible. Money is often seen as a reason or used as an excuse for not being able to change; for remaining 'stuck' in a job, a relationship, a home that you would prefer to leave. This surprisingly can come from having either a lack of, *or* an excess of, financial wealth.

In fact, the main capital for bringing about change is *not* financial capital; it is *intellectual* capital: your thoughts, your will, your knowledge, your determination.

The converse of not having enough money could therefore be translated into not having enough brainpower; but we *know* that we each have enough brainpower. None of us uses more than one per cent of the total capacity of our brain *in a lifetime*. Besides, most of the multi-billionaires on this planet started with nothing and used their imagination and all their qualities as positive Change Makers to bring about a very positive financial change.

■ Welcome to the Century of Intellectual Capital and Innovation

At the fifth annual conference of the United Nations on the Reinvention (*Change*) of Government and Innovation (*Creativity*), President Vicente Fox of Mexico told 10,000 international delegates in Mexico City in November of 2003 that these concepts were so important that the twenty-first century should be proclaimed 'the Century of Intellectual Capital and Innovation'.

On the converse side of this coin, having too much money can be a demotivator. This occurs when money is seen as the prime goal in its own right.

When success is achieved, it can seem as if no further effort is required. In this situation it is important to realize that:

Money is like a circulation system, a form of energy. It is to be used and renewed.

This is why you will often find extremely wealthy individuals begin to adjust their vision over time, from the accumulation of financial wealth to the distribution of that wealth for the realization of other more significant changes, including education or health and welfare foundations and charities.

If financial concerns are dominating your life to such an extent that you can genuinely no longer function in a balanced way, you need to include a Financial Advisor and other financially adept mentors as part of your Change Manager group.

Start Mind Mapping your way to a Vision of positive change. You may have skills, talents or capital assets that you haven't considered. You may work up to more radical action – such as relocation in order to broaden your options. Whatever your current situation, there *is* a solution. You need to stop repeating any negative behaviour that might be making your situation worse. Visualize your goal and make plans to move actively *towards* it in Meta-Positive fashion, one step at a time.

Money may frequently seem important, but it is the resource that matters *least* in the achievement of our endeavours. Of far more importance is the way in which we focus our thoughts and our actions to optimize our strengths and abilities and to achieve our personal Vision.

■ You can change the world

> *'I wanted to change the world. But I have found that the only thing one can be sure of changing is oneself.'*
> **Aldous Huxley**

When I was Mind-Mapping the plan for *Embracing Change*, I was reminded of the above quote by Huxley. Take a moment to consider what he is saying. Do the words have resonance for you? If so, do not be persuaded! This oft-quoted concept is compelling in its emphasis and its simplicity; but I want to challenge the premise by pointing out that it is in fact wrong. It is inside out, and back-to-front!

Huxley (and others who have said similar things) made a mistake in thinking that has led many people to despair – because in making the mistaken assumption that in changing 'only' themselves they are *limiting* their influence, they presume they are unable to influence or change anything else, including the world, for the better. In fact, the opposite is true.

The crux of the matter is that if you change *yourself*, by definition you *do* change the world. Not only are you changing anyway, not only are you going to change anyway, but you are going to change *every second for the rest of your life*. There is no limit to the potential of your influence: a much more truthful and positive result.

You therefore have a dramatic choice to make, which in times of great pain and personal pressure can feel like a mountain that you have been asked to climb. Do you want to change yourself and the world for the worse? Or do your want to change yourself and the world for the better?

The choice of change is not yours.

The choice of the direction of change *is* yours.

Influence

Tiny Atomy
Dropped into the Pond
of the Cosmos

Even *my* ripples

Wave

To the ends
Of the Universe.

*If we don't change,
we don't grow.
If we don't grow,
we aren't really living.*

Gail Sheehy, *Passages* (1974)

Chapter 9
Life changes: how to use a change journal

❏ Buzan's Tools for Transformation: 7. Your Change Journal

Throughout history, Change Thinkers and Change Makers of all disciplines – great scientists, great artists, great inventors – have kept notebooks and used sketches and illustrations to bring form to their ideas and to move closer towards the realization of their Goals. Interestingly, many of the shapes and structures used to express their ideas and imaginings are reminiscent of Mind Maps. Sketches and notebooks form a record of the creative process, an archive of memory, and can be a lodestone to check personal development and as a reference by which to chart the rest of the journey of discovery.

The seventh Tool for Transformation introduces you to a unique form of notebook that will help you to put form and substance to your ideas. This multi-dimensional and change-making notebook will be your Change Journal.

■ Mind Map review

You already know that, like a journey planner, a Mind Map will:

1. Give you an overview of the 'big picture'; the scope of the terrain that you have to navigate.

2. Enable you to plan your journey and to make choices en route.

3. Let you know where you are, where you are going, and where you have been.

4. Gather and hold large amounts of data.

5. Encourage daydreaming and problem solving by looking for creative pathways.

6. Enable you to be extremely efficient.

7. Be enlightening, inspiring and enjoyable to look at, muse over and remember.

A single, focused Mind Map will clarify your Vision and provide a visual record of the TEFCAS process, by:

1. Showing how and where you have Tried.

2. Painting clearly the Events that have followed.

3. Providing Feedback to enable you to …

4. Check the information provided and encourage you to…

5. Adjust and progress towards …

6. Achieving future Success in pursuit of your Goal.

If a single Mind Map is such a powerful tool, imagine how inspiring a sequence of Mind Maps will be. They will aid in the creation and continuation of your ideas, they will encourage the ongoing creative vitality that it will nurture and develop your progression towards your Vision.

Your Change Journal will become a permanent record of your Change Mind Maps. Your Change Journal will provide a visual and multi-dimensional memory of your Change Journey that will enable you to see at a glance how far you have travelled; how your attitude has transformed; the extent to which you are driving your own destiny; and how successful you are being in planning your own life path.

Buzan's Tools for Transformation
7. Your Change Journal

Just as Mind Mapping is the perfect way of seeing your ideas come to life and having the freedom to add to them, Mind Maps in journal form provide a means of taking stock, to see how you are progressing on your path to achieving your Vision of Change.

If you ever feel that you have become 'stuck' and are 'right back to square one', a glance through your journal will enable you to see that that is far from the truth.

How does this work?

Your Mind Map Change Journal incorporates *all* the Buzan Tools for Transformation in ongoing Mind Map form:

■ Your Change Journal, and Vision and Focus

Every Mind Map has at its centre a Vision, a Goal, a main focal point. If you have prepared twenty Change Mind Maps, each will have a different focal point. Putting them all together in journal form will allow you to:

- ■ Look over the results of all your creative thoughts.
- ■ Decide what your main Change Vision is, by taking a look at the results of each of the Mind Maps.
- ■ Add any additional thoughts, words, feelings, or other aspects.

Do you want to see the Big Picture?

Create a NEW Mind Map for Change that will incorporate ALL the key factors you have identified so far. Each of the Mind Maps will be a branch on the new Mind Map. Add a few empty branches, to encourage your brain to add further ideas.

Do you need to clarify which of your priorities should be your primary goal?

Put your SELF in the centre of the Mind Map. Ask yourself:

Who do I want to be?

Who am I now?

What are my strengths and weaknesses?

What is my primary goal?

What do I need to change to transform myself?

Who will I need to support and help me to achieve my goal?

Once you have completed the process, WEIGHT the results (see page 103) – and Believe your conclusions!

■ Your Change Journal and TEFCAS

The Change Journal is the Mind Mapped record of your TEFCAS process of change and successes.

As well as the recording of your Trials and Events, the Mind Maps in your Change Journal will provide a true Feedback device. They are your Checking tool, as well as the thinking tool that allows you to plan your Adjustment appropriately. They will show you whether you have remained Focused on your main Goal; they will show you whether you have Tried to bring about appropriate Events that kept you on track, or whether you have been 'off target' with your actions.

If you Check and Adjust your response in line with your Mind Map Feedback, in a way that moves you *towards* your goal, you *will* achieve Success and your journey will come a wonderful full circle; i.e. If you have remained 'on track' towards your original Vision, your final Success Mind Map will ideally reflect your original Goal Mind Map, and the enhancements will be the result of progressing through the process of TEFCAS. You will have achieved congruence.

■ Your Change Journal and Mind Maps

Creating a series of Mind Maps based on the themes in each of the chapters of this book will reflect back to you how you experience the world. In taking stock of how you experience and interpret the world, you can see where your life is out of balance, where you want to enhance your experiences of life, and how to plan and prioritize to bring about change in the future.

Once you have mapped these out, it is crucial that you prioritize them and anchor them in time-based goals. By so doing, they immediately become achievable because you have placed them in a time-based context. The next step is choosing to Try for the change.

■ Your Change Journal and Meta-Positive Thinking

Your Change Journal will also, importantly, incorporate the principles of Meta-Positive Thought. You will be concentrating on the Positive, on your Successes, as a method of personal motivation, and as a way of dealing with whatever movements *away* from your goal might have occurred in the process.

Your Mind Maps will enable you to be both objective and positive at the same time. Objectivity is neither positive nor negative; it is Absolute. It is The Truth. A Mind Map, because it is objective, will therefore deliver to you the Truth. Your Mind Map will allow you to see the *whole picture* in a clear, objective, comprehensive and enlightened manner – incorporating the Good and the Bad – and even the Ugly!

This is why your Meta-Positive Attitude is important. A Mind Map will encourage you to face your reality as you would look at objective scientific pure data, and say to yourself: 'Well, that is where I am *at this moment* in the ongoing experiment of change. That is the Truth.'

The Truth may not always feel comfortable, and it is important to ask yourself in a Meta-Positive frame of mind: 'Where is the next *Positive* step to be taken towards the goal of Success?' The way in which you react to that question will result from your Meta-Positive Thinking.

The Mind Map will become your guide, your shepherd, in helping you to achieve this process. The Change Journal will become the perfect positive Voice of Change coach. It will always tell you the Truth; it will always give you honest Feedback; it will always show you the best next Change Step to take you further towards your goal.

■ Your Change Journal and your Change Masters

When embarking on a journey or learning a new skill, it is natural to draw upon the knowledge and expertise of others whose opinions we respect as experts in that field – to enable the best possible decision, and the most enjoyable or expert result. The same applies when assessing your Mind Maps in Change Journal form.

■ Refer to your 'Inner' Change Masters to gain inspiration, motivation and new perspective from the approaches of great geniuses of the past.

■ Refer to 'Outer' Change Masters who know you best, who have expertise in the area you are considering and can add insight to your situation.

■ Use your own mind to look at the situation from the perspective of others. Draw a Mind Map of actions that your Change Masters might recommend – and review the outcomes.

■ The Purpose of a Change Journal

The joy of a Change Journal is that it is multi-faceted in purpose. It can be used to monitor time and events, but more importantly it can be used to explore and chart your short, mid- and long-term dreams and ambitions.

Some may treat it as a diary to be used in daily response to events that have happened and as a means of planning ahead. Others may prefer to use it as an occasional tool to focus on particular projects and ambitions, to ensure that you are keeping on track or to TEFCAS positive progress.

You will gauge enormous benefit from your Mind Maps if you review them periodically, and create a Change Journal in which to explore your ideas, plans, dreams and visions. It is an ideal method for measuring your progress in a powerful and visible way, and also allows you to add perspective to the past – because each time you revisit your earlier Mind Maps you will interpret them in a different way.

By embarking on keeping a Change Journal, you are creating a visual record of your immediate feelings, and taking the first practical step towards turning your vision of the future into a practical reality.

Life-planning divisions

Your Change Journal can help you to keep track of the different aspects of your life. In order to keep the mind focused, it is best to keep your ideas honed to the basics.

The most useful are:

1. Health & Fitness
2. Friends & Relationships
3. Leisure & Creativity
4. Wealth
5. Work
6. Home and Family
7. Education & Learning

Why not prepare a Change Map for each of these areas in order to 'jump start' your journal and to give yourself a Starting Point for Change?

There are many ways to organize your thoughts in Change Journal form.

■ You may like to organize them in a ring binder, thematically.
■ You may want to devote a wall of your home to a multi-dimensional frieze that radiates Mind Map ideas.
■ You may want to frame them, or keep the current one in view while keeping the others in tubes or boxes.

Whatever works for you, you have the flexibility and choice to do.

■ It is important to ensure that you date and sign each one as you complete it.

■ It is important that they are kept in an orderly way that makes sense of the ideas and the subject matter.

This is because as you refer back to one or more of your Mind Maps, you will want to know the context and the subsequent progression.

Because of the dynamic nature of the Mind Map process, by the time you have completed your ambition, the next change path will already have presented itself. You will see change appear before your eyes and in anticipating it, will be able to grow with it and flow with it.

As you make the Change Journal part of your regular activity, so you will begin to see your ideas take shape, progress, emerge on the page.

Your Change Challenge will in time become a Change in Progress and then a Change Achieved.

■ The benefits of your Change Journal

Your Change Journal:

■ will provide a comprehensive life-management tool for past, present and future.

■ will enhance your powers of self-analysis, problem-solving and personal organization.

■ will provide a visually attractive record of your Change path.

■ over a period of time will enable you to identify your personal patterns of behaviour and observe long-term trends.

■ allows you to follow the TEFCAS model and move forward towards Success.

■ is a dramatic and colourful representation of Meta-Positive Thinking in Practice.

■ enables you to see the impact that your Change Masters have had in your life.

■ is easy to use and puts you in control of your life.

■ provides a visual record of your life as a positive Change Thinker and Change Maker.

■ The Change Journal in action

A Change Journal is a highly positive and dynamic tool for change. In this section we are focusing on a more challenging area of life to demonstrate that especially in times of personal adversity and aloneness, the Buzan approach in the form of a Change Journal can transform heart-breaking situations into enriching ones.

Waiting for an illness to take its natural course, particularly if your loved one is suffering, is one of the most difficult and challenging experiences anyone is likely to be faced with in life. It is also a time when the phases of Loss are most apparent. (See Chapter 12.)

When you consider the inevitable, you feel shattered, rent asunder, ripped apart. That is why those living closely with death every day are likely to take solace in their daily routine and humour to see them through. A sense of the absurd can be a powerful tool for positive change.

Friends and relatives who are slightly distanced from the situation can find it harder to come to terms with the inevitable than the one/s who is/are living through it. This is because the person who is ill is living 'in the moment', whereas those who are trying to protect themselves from the inevitable are either denying the pain of the future, or feeling overwhelmed by memories of the past.

In this instance, the *choice* you *do* have is how you are going to deal with impending, frightening and often mortifying change, and help others deal with the situation. For example, you might ask yourself whether you have become caught up in your own personal pain and despair at the expense of making the final days of the stricken individual as beautiful as possible; on the other hand, you may have become so devoted to the person who is ill that you have lost balance in your own life. You need to keep planning for your own future while helping others to come to terms with theirs.

If you can find a balance, and achieve a positive approach, you will effect positive change and a more loving and embracing atmosphere for your loved one in the last days of life. You will also have given yourself and others positive memories to carry for the rest of your life around this event.

A crisis may bring people together and lead to new depths of relationship, but it can also create tensions and strains. Some families are able to support one another through crisis but this is not always possible and conflicts can emerge. If you find yourself in conflict with others in your family, or close circle, remember that they, too, are in pain, and are having trouble facing their fears, just as you are.

Remember:

The *anticipation* of the event drives the fear, even more than the event itself.

If you are focused externally and positively, your own angst or *Weltschmerz* [world sorrow] will be lessened, you will be healthier and happier; you will therefore be better able to help others to become stronger in the face of personal agony. You will have strengthened your internal fibre (although it may not feel that way at the time) and influenced others in a way that in future they too may be able to deal with such change in a way that makes the best of a painful situation.

■ Joy's story

Joy was out of the country on business when her mother Hannah became seriously ill and was rushed unwillingly to hospital. Joy returned to witness a veritable nightmare of checks and tests, which were threatening Hannah's dignity, self-respect and her fighting spirit. The doctors were recommending investigative surgery – but with no conclusive proof that they knew what was amiss.

'I was faced with a situation requiring a million decisions, but without any real information.' Joy told me. 'The doctor was saying, "We *think* your mother should be operated on." I said, "You only *think* she should be operated on? My mother is nearly 90; she may not *survive* an operation."'

Joy felt pressurized to make a fast decision, but not informed. She had to balance putting her mother through the trauma of an operation against the uncertainty of resolving her condition via other means. The doctor made it clear that if she turned down the chance of the operation, she was on her own. The responsibility was *all hers*. Joy wasn't getting clear answers to her questions and was concerned at the side effects of Hannah's heavy medication. She made the decision to take her home.

'I had never looked after anyone who was very sick before,' Joy told me.

'My life became 24-hour care; the house was turned into a hospital environment. Trying to maintain my mother's dignity in the light of the reversal of our roles was hard. I just keep thinking, how do we manage this graciously? The trouble is when you're in this kind of situation, there isn't a minute to stop and think. Trying to gain perspective was difficult.

'In times of crisis you are forced to go right back to basics – and all the busying makes the function of stopping to plan extremely difficult. You get really tired; become totally exhausted. How do you recharge? Because there isn't a moment in that moment.

'I would create many, many mini Mind Maps – as a way of releasing my anger and my frustration. *It's not fair! One minute happy, one minute sad. Where do I go for information? Where do I get help?* I would get it all out, and down on to a piece of paper – and then just screw it up and throw it away because once it was out it was dealt with. Then I could concentrate on "the 5 per cent" I could do *something* about.

'I was trying to peel away my emotions and just look at the facts, while also asking what does my gut level tell me? It's very important to listen to your intuition. What happens is the little voice gets overwhelmed by the emotion and the logic and so you sometimes go off on a wrong tack because you're listening too much to either the emotional or the logical voice.'I made Plans - looking at every possibility. I'd look at "If that, then what, if this, then what... can I handle that? Yes, No. If not, what do I need to do if I can't handle that." It was always a series of cause and effect.

'If I couldn't see a positive outcome, the question became: What are the things that I can do to try to make the situation as good as possible, given certain parameters? How can I try to come up with plans?

'My strategy was to mini Mind Map all of the options – very, very quickly, extremely basically, in the minutes between other tasks.

'On some days there were rays of hope, and then her condition would deteriorate again. I didn't know whether I was watching her recover or watching her die. The deterioration would feel 50 times worse, because we had begun to be hopeful. So there was a yo-yo effect– each little glimmer of hope meaning that we almost sank deeper afterwards. Instead of being inspiring, the success almost undermined us ... Could we go through this again?'

In a desperate moment Joy found herself exclaiming: 'Just how much more can I take?' This very moment of despair brought humour and a 'paradigm shift' – a completely fresh way of viewing the situation: 'Wrong question!' she said. 'If I keep asking how much more can I take, the answer will be – More, of course! So, I declared more positively: "Thank you, that's enough!"' And with some further Meta-Positive Thinking, positive planning and plenty of TEFCAS trials – the onslaught stopped.

As the weeks progressed, Hannah's recovery improved to the extent that they even managed to celebrate her 90th birthday with friends.

■ Times of extreme challenge

During the course of Joy's period of crisis, her Mind Map Journal became a lifeline.

- ■ The process of Mind Mapping helped her to transform her reactive state to a proactive one.
- ■ Mind Mapping helped her to transform a crisis into a period of intimacy and growth, where she learnt more about her own capacity to manage, and became even closer to her mother as they worked together to deal with the situation.
- ■ The illness, rather than being negative, was eventually transformed into a positive experience by the nurturing responses of those around her.
- ■ Her awareness of TEFCAS meant that she was able to see when and how her efforts were producing results.
- ■ The sense of control that was generated by the Mind Maps fed her attitude in a way that helped her to remain positive in adversity.

Joy's account shows what others who have experienced times of extreme challenge have observed: that there are many personal discoveries and qualities that are possible to gain from a period of profound change that enable you to regain balance:

- ■ You realize how flexible you can be.
- ■ You realize you can have dignity in any situation.

■ You become more compassionate and develop empathy for other people's suffering.

■ You get more and more confidence in your strength because you come to know that you can handle whatever life throws at you; you are no longer so vulnerable or raw.

■ You discover the level of persistence that you have.

■ You keep going past when you think you will fold; even if you do fold momentarily, you unfold and carry on again.

■ You discover the power of humour to get you through difficult moments and out the other side.

■ You discover the amazing gift of love and support from friends and acquaintances.

■ Material wealth is put in perspective.

■ Many discover the power of their spiritual connection.

■ You discover the ability of the brain to shift in adjustment according to the situation.

■ You are likely to develop patience.

■ You may learn to detach from the outcome, over which you may have no control.

■ You learn to let go of your personal needs out of recognition of what is best for the other person.

So even in seemingly negative scenarios, remember that the gifts you will receive when you are able to gain perspective will outweigh the upset of the moment.

From Joy's story you can see that using the life journal in such situations can help you gain a greater, common, more stable and calmer perspective on a situation which otherwise might seem utterly out of control.

■ Max's story

Max was born and grew up by the sea in Canada. He had lived and breathed boats and sailing since he was a small boy, and even as an adult, while earning significant sums as a City broker, he escaped each weekend to the coast to indulge his passion for the ocean.

He was introduced to Mind Maps at a business conference in New York and found himself doodling in the form of Mind Maps with increasing regularity, but yachts rather than finance were frequently the central image. He tucked these away, considering them self-indulgent musings – but, he said, 'I began to dream about sailing, and being by the coast. Although I loved what I did and enjoyed the City lifestyle, I knew in my heart it wasn't for me long term.'

At the age of 27 he took the decision to move out of his City role and to work as an investor for a smaller organization close to where he went sailing. He had expected to enjoy combining working within a less stressful environment with having more time to sail in the evenings and at weekends – but it wasn't enough.

Max was focused more firmly than he realized on the Big Vision.

He retrieved his Mind Maps and considered the recurring themes that were presenting themselves. He combined them consciously in a Master Mind Map and then weighted the results. His conclusions? His age, enthusiasm, desire and motivation were all guiding him towards exploring a career change. Finance was not a concern, and he was free to Focus his attention on making a move towards the Big Vision.

Just three months after relocating he resigned his position and signed up to re-train as a skipper. His Mind Map Journal is on board with him and is now playing a conscious part in charting new territories.

Max's story demonstrates that keeping a Mind Map Journal can be an invaluable way of spotting underlying trends and desires that you may be denying to yourself.

It is also the perfect Tool for transforming your outdated present into a positive plan of action for attaining your preferred future.

In summary – the Change Journal is the externalizing of your thought processes. The Change Journal allows you externalize your thoughts, dreams, ambitions and problems in Mind Map form; to organize them sequentially, to manage yourself in time rather than frantically trying to manage time; to have a daily support for reviewing the past and planning for your future; to file and mark those things which are important and require your ongoing attention;

to act as your coach, guide and friend in times of great excitement or deep stress; and most important of all to give you control over the changes you intend and need to bring about in times of urgency, crisis and dynamic development.

Name Me

When All
Is Still
I am Still

When Forces
Greater than me
Attack,
I Move
And stay Still

What fells others
Mightier than Me
Does not fell me

I am Your True
Shelter in a Storm

Your

....

You will find the answer on page 264.

PART THREE

Life planning

To see a World in a Grain of Sand
And a Heaven in a Wild Flower
Hold Infinity in the palm of your hand
And Eternity in an hour

William Blake

Chapter 10
Changing your life balance

❏ Take stock of your life balance

❏ Have a Big Vision

❏ Manage yourself in time

❏ Rebalance life and restore health

The previous chapters have encouraged you to take stock of your life to date, to review your goals, and to gain a greater sense of who you are and where you are headed. Now is the time to look at the balance of your life. This section of the book focuses on Life Balance and will explore how Buzan's Tools for Transformation can be applied over time.

As you journey through life you will encounter a series of life milestones. The importance and value of these will differ for each individual, and each person will embrace change with a different emphasis and focus. One fact is constant: with each milestone, the priorities and balance of your life *will* change.

By maintaining or achieving balance, the new change in your life will be an important landmark around and over which the river of your life will happily flow. Whether the change is a positive challenge or an awkward obstacle, you will, with your ongoing energy, make it part of your life.

■ A Frog's Tale

If a frog is placed in cold water, which is then heated up fast, it will jump out very quickly in order to protect itself from pain and certain death.

If, however, the frog is placed in cold water and the water is then heated very slowly, the frog will not notice the change in temperature; it will become gradually drowsy and will eventually allow itself to be boiled alive.

In the second scenario the frog has become too comfortable in the context of the continuing minor change and does not realize that there will come a critical point at which the change can be catastrophic. There are times when immediate action and a change of behaviour are required in order to avert catastrophe.

■ A question of balance

If you do not keep in balance, you are in danger of becoming like the frog in the story above. The change from balance to imbalance will not occur overnight; it can be a slow, gradual habit of change. You may not notice that your life has become uncomfortable or intolerable until it has reached almost boiling point.

Jilted Frog

Change creeps up
like a hunter in the night;
With stealthy paws
kneads the drowsy
mind
to numbness;

Kills
With increasing Warmth
Disguised
As Love

When you are going through a big life change you will be able to cope better and be optimistic if you:

- Make time to maintain your physical and mental health.
- Remember the importance of Lifelong Learning and Keep Alert to the possibility of learning new things.
- Nurture your friendships and family relationships.
- Have plenty of mini breaks, where you do something totally different. Breaks and a change of pace are vital to enable the brain to absorb data and to regenerate.
- Have the appropriate amount of sleep. More than five hours of sleep a night and less than ten will restore your energy levels and enable your body and brain to work to the optimum.

'Easy for you to say,' you may cry, 'but *I haven't got time because …'*

My new project is due to be launched in three months' time – it's vital that I focus 100 per cent of my time on its development.

Not true! You *should* be 100 per cent focused on achieving that Vision but that is not the same as spending 100 per cent of your time working solidly and *solely* upon it. You'll feel more energetic and your brain will create far fresher ideas about the product launch if you take time out to find out what others in your life are doing. Taking a break will enable the brain to work more effectively and take you further towards achieving your Goal.

I am juggling management responsibilities at work with the demands of being a parent. How can I find time to learn new things?

Easily! Realize that the object of your Focus needs to become Your Needs. Organize your personal time with the rigour you apply to your office life. Ensure you reserve at least one night a week and at least 20 minutes a day for You.

My new baby has changed my life. By the time I've finished feeding, changing and bathing him, I'm exhausted and no longer have time to see friends, to go out, to pursue my interests.

Stop your new bad habits before they become entrenched! When *will* you begin to see your friends if not now? New babies are highly portable and they sleep a lot of the time. Keep essential baby paraphernalia to a minimum and take the baby with you when you go out. Enlist help from Change Makers – family, godparents, or other new parents – who will grow to know your baby and who will then grow to know your child.

By the time I get home at the end of a twelve-hour day I'm too exhausted to join a gym or to keep fit.

Danger! Your life is significantly out of balance. Take this book seriously: use the Tools for Transformation. They will help you to regain life balance and restore your health.

■ Changing in time

The concept of Time provides us with many instances of irony and paradox but nothing else offers us a greater barometer for measuring change.

Managing Time is an aspect of life that overwhelms many people and prevents them from fulfilling their true potential. This is hardly surprising as Time has been managing itself for a minimum of fifteen billion years without any management by us! The traditional concept of Time Management is a misnomer. What is essential in bringing about appropriate change is that we manage ourselves *in* time. In managing ourselves, we need simultaneously to consider the past, the present and the future.

The crucial factor is to plan for the 'medium' term in our short- medium- and long-term objectives.

For example, if your long-term (annual) sales target is £600,000 it makes sense to divide it into twelve so that you know your short-term (monthly) sales target is £50,000. In order to achieve that long-term goal, however, the figure you are really focusing on is the medium-term (quarterly) sales target of £150,000. If you are too focused on the short term you will lose sight of the big picture. If you are too focused on the long term there is a danger that you will not plan efficiently and will not put in place the stepping-stones to achieve your goal.

You need to Mind Map your strategy with your medium-term goal at the centre and then apply the TEFCAS model, one step at a time, through each short-term goal to reach it.

■ Keeping both eyes on the game

To accomplish a Vision in terms of short-, medium- and long-term goals, the constant goal you must have is the Big Vision.

Think of the power and focus of the cheetah. The cheetah is the fastest animal on earth, able to achieve a speed of 70mph. The cheetah's Vision is the antelope, which is its method of survival.

If you look at a cheetah in pursuit of its prey, you see a body in total, absolute motion, all parts moving with astonishing grace and elegance and with extreme extension and contraction. However, the one piece of that body to remain totally and relatively still when it's hurtling forward at speed is the head. That head is locked onto its target just like a radar-guided missile and wherever the antelope twists and turns, the cheetah's head and the eyes are focused totally upon it. It is almost as if they are attached by some invisible cord. It is only with this fixated vision that the cheetah is able to accomplish its goals. If its vision for one moment steers away from its goal, it will hurtle all its extraordinary energy in the wrong direction.

Exactly the same principle applies to your major Vision. Your internal eye, your mind's eye needs to stay focused on that Big Vision to enable your mind and body's total efforts and actions to be directed towards your Goal. The

short-term and mid-term Goals are mini-Visions on the way to the Big Vision.

If a cheetah had a Big Vision it would be to ensure the lifelong, ongoing supply of antelope. Its mid-term goal would be to ensure that there was enough antelope to feed its young; and the short-term goal would be to capture the particular antelope on which it is focusing.

It is a salutary truth that if you mismanage your opportunities for change as you progress along your life path, the possibility of achieving the goals you have established for yourself will recede as the time apportioned to you decreases. It is therefore essential to be conscious of where you are on your life path, to be clear about your personal Vision and to review your goals on a regular basis.

If you manage yourself in the river of time you will make sure that you bring about changes at appropriate junctures and in an appropriate rhythm.

■ Are you off-balance?

There are many indicators that life is out of balance and these tend to be the same indicators as those of stress.

There will be:

- ■ Increased irritability
- ■ An increasing lack of consideration for all others except yourself
- ■ Lack of self-care
- ■ An increasing weakness of the immune system
- ■ A tendency to get colds or minor ailments
- ■ Signs of the beginning of more major ailments and breakdown
- ■ A tendency to resort to smoking, alcohol or other hard or soft drugs
- ■ The dissolution of family relationships
- ■ The dissolution of social relationships
- ■ A frustration with work and professional life
- ■ Loss of memory
- ■ General dis-ease
- ■ General dis-satisfaction

Noticing any of these symptoms is an Event, an indication that you are changing *away* from your goal. Each symptom will provide you with Feedback, showing you that you need to Take Action to stop doing what you've been doing and Adjust your future behaviour.

■ **Taking stock of your life balance**

A Change Programme that improves your Life Balance will progress through the following stages:

1. **Method** Use TEFCAS to gain Feedback on your current behaviour.
2. **Vision** Envision yourself as a balanced and healthy individual.
3. **Plan** Objectively Mind Map your current situation and create another Mind Map of Mind Maps, to focus on your short-, medium- and long-term goals.
4. **Prioritize** Decide upon which of your Goals is the most important and which direction you need to take in order to achieve it.
5. **Weight** Determine the level of importance of each of your priorities.
6. **Think** Focus on developing Meta-Positive Thinking Habits.
7. **Commit** Positively commit to taking the action that is going to direct you closer towards your medium-term goal.
8. **Act** Use all the Tools for Transformation, beginning with the Try of TEFCAS, to launch yourself towards achieving your new goals.
9. **Record** Record your achievements in further Mind Maps in Journal form. (See Chapter 9.)
10. **Persist** Repeat and repeat! Again and again and again – beyond your normal comfort zone – as you move closer and closer towards achieving your objective.

■ **Using TEFCAS for life balance**

When taking stock of your own ongoing life balance, Check whether the Feedback resulting from your ongoing Trys and Events is taking you towards or away from the Success you aim to achieve.

Remember:

Try➤ Event ➤ Feedback ➤ Check ➤ Adjust ➤ Success ➤

Ask yourself Feedback questions, such as:

■ Am I spending a disproportionate amount of time at work?

■ Have I seen my children/family within the last three days/weeks/ months?

■ Am I maintaining and improving my health?

■ When was the last time I had a Fitness Assessment to check my stamina, my muscular strength, my flexibility and my overall state of medical well-being?

■ Am I getting enough sleep?

■ Am I happy fundamentally with myself and the way my life is progressing?

■ Am I allocating time to spend not only with my family but also my friends and wider social acquaintances?

■ Am I including within my constant Self-Check a balance between learning new things and applying to my life what I *have* learnt?

■ Do I devote time to spend with myself alone, and do I enjoy my own company at that time?

■ Have I developed addictive behaviour – excessive drinking, shopping, eating chocolate, smoking, gambling?

■ Have I become a TV couch-potato *every* night?

■ Am I comfortable in my own skin?

■ Do I feel that I am managing change in an effective manner?

To achieve Life Balance is ideally to reach a situation in which all areas of your life are humming with energy and productivity, while at the same time you as an individual are congruent with yourself, happy with your state of being and progressing in a way that you would wish to progress.

Using a Mind Map to assess life balance

Take a few moments to create a **Whole Life Mind Map**. This needn't be complex. Put your SELF at the centre and include basic categories such as: Home, Friends, Love and Sex, Family, Children, Work, Hobbies, Creativity, Finances, Health and Fitness, Spirit – or others that suit your needs.

To maintain healthy balance it is essential that throughout periods of time where the emphasis of your life changes you keep the overall balance stable. As one branch of your life grows, take care to keep the other basic branches strong also, so you do not neglect the roots of your stability that nourish your ongoing growth.

■ Weighting your feedback

A beneficial way to lend more precision to the change Feedback provided by your Mind Map is to weight the results by level of importance. By this I mean simply to grade your Feedback on scale of 0–10 in relation to your goal.

10 = High: you feel positive about this aspect; all is well/ good.

0 = Low: you feel negative about this aspect; all is not well/ it is bad.

For example: *How is your health developing?*

■ Perfectly and wonderfully would prompt a '10'.

■ If you are overweight, lethargic and developing negative addictions, you would consider the answer '0'.

Once you have completed this exercise, add up the scores and consider the Feedback they give you. Use this numerical intelligence to help your intuition guide you toward focusing on the next step in your change process.

The highest and lowest numbers will obviously be the ones that guide you towards deciding your next priorities for achieving Balance. Aim to maintain and use your strengths to help you to bolster the areas that are somewhat lagging in your ongoing change process.

■ Introducing the Mind Map change wheel

To explore this further I encourage you to use the Mind Map Change Wheel. It is a Mind Map Matrix designed so that you can see 'at a glance' whether your life is in balance. This invaluable tool was created by my colleague and Change Master, Vanda North.

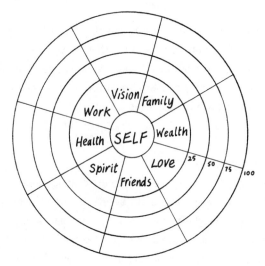

Imagine that this is the wheel of your life. Referring back to your Whole Life Mind Map, you are going to colour in each of the sections to a level that shows the degree to which the area dominates your life. Those areas of your life that are in balance will be shaded roughly to the same level. Others may be barely completed, or may extend beyond the circumference of the circle.

Once complete, imagine the effect if your Matrix were the front wheel of a bicycle you are riding down a road. Would you enjoy a smooth ride? Would you be jolted uncomfortably by the bumps in the wheel but still manage an interesting journey? Or would its uneven shape mean you would either not get started or would you find yourself a heap in the road?

 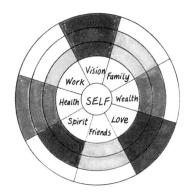

The wheel is a metaphor for your Life Balance at the moment and the bicycle represents your life path. You will be able to tell from the level of discomfort whether you will pedal freely or struggle to your destination, and where it is necessary to make immediate adjustments.

Your priorities are likely to change at key points in your life. When, for example, your children grow up and leave home the branch for Children will (and *should*) take less priority. This does not mean that you no longer love your children or that they are no longer a part of your life; it means that part of your life's work is complete, it is time to let them 'fly' and to develop their own life path and for you to delight in that transition. It is an opportunity for other branches on your own Mind Map tree of life to grow, for you to 'branch out' towards: travel, self-development, continuing self-education. You will begin to see and experience your life anew.

The Family branch of your Mind Map will diminish over time in terms of children, but may well expand in time in relation to your partner, your elderly parents or grandchildren. Your Health branch will remain a constant; your Creativity and Hobbies branches will remain constant.

Your Friends branch will change, but should be constantly nourished and kept growing. Throughout life it is very important to anchor change by guaranteeing that as you progress you continue to enjoy social interaction and friends of all different ages and types, so that you enrich your enjoyment and understanding of the world with a constant flow of human beings who will massage your social health.

■ Being out of balance

There are of course many occasions when being Out of Balance is a very good thing. All events, all learning experiences, if used appropriately, if used as opportunities for learning, will in the long run strengthen you. Certainly if you are 'in love', in the throes of new parenthood, starting an exciting new job or enjoying the joy of a sporting success, having your life turned upside-down and inside-out in an extreme and unbalanced way can be an ecstatic and heady experience. As anyone who has experienced the limelight of fame will tell you, however, when the giddy heights beckon, having strong roots upon which you can rely becomes ever more important in order to keep your Vision clear and to help you retain your balance.

■ Using Meta-Positive thinking to regain life balance

That which does not destroy us makes us stronger.
Otto von Bismarck

There are times when you may plateau in a particular state of change. Thus if you are involved in an exciting project, you might feel that progress is stagnant. If you have lost your job or have suffered a bereavement, it may seem that your life in the short term has lost its purpose or has no meaning.

If at these moments you feel the tentacles of victim mentality taking hold of your freedom of thought, *beware* of the temptation to give up your facility as a Change Thinker. This is a particular danger if you have suffered a whole gamut of catastrophic change over which you have had little control. You may feel exhausted, your financial resources may be diminishing, your energy could be at a low ebb, you are tempted to feel that you have been abandoned to the twists and turns of 'fate' and that you just can't cope any more.

Having reached this point in *Embracing Change*, you will know that you do *always* have choice, that even at your lowest ebb, your body and brain do always have the capacity to adapt creatively and change *positively*. You may want to Adjust your network of Change Thinkers and Change Makers to help you to understand your Feedback; you may need to Adjust your Vision of change and your ultimate goal of Success in response to the Event. You may need courage to face this Adjustment – but you can do it and you will then be changing in a direction of your choice.

This is the ideal moment to create a Mind Map. You may think you are lost or are making slow progress; not true – refocus and re-energize your Vision and you will quickly start to move forward again. Get those ideas down on paper. Don't worry if your thoughts feel absurd – just keep them flowing.

Once you have completed the task – and you may want to tackle it in several brain-bursts of time over several days - take a good look at those areas of your talents that you may have allowed to lie fallow; look for the inner creative you that has been sleeping through your period of radical change. Assess and weigh up the results. Decide which of the ideas or themes is to be your next goal. Put this at the centre of a new Mind Map and this time add more proactive headings such as: When?, How?, Why?, Where?, Who?, What?

Commit to take this action forward, and use TEFCAS to assess your progress and Meta-Positive Thinking to develop new habits of thought and behaviour. There is only one route for you to go: upwards towards positive change and success.

■ Change addiction

Although Change is positive and inevitable, there is one form of change that you should view with caution. Let me introduce here the concept of the Change Addict.

The Change Addict is one who reacts impulsively, who changes for the sake of change without considering the short-, medium- and long-term effects that those changes are going to bring about in his life. It is very common for the Change Addict to develop change addiction as a method of escaping responsibility or escaping situations that are too painful to face.

In personal relationships change addiction may develop following the break-up of a relationship that has been particularly intense or meaningful. Anyone who has ever been especially hurt by the ending of a relationship will know that you may carry the fear of inevitable pain into your next relationship. As soon the next relationship threatens to become as serious as the one that ended, your mind will trigger the association of love and hurt. At that point you have the choice of whether to take the risk and move closer to the greater goal of deeper love and affection or whether to distance yourself.

There is a danger that you may terminate the relationship or shut off your feelings in order to prevent the possibility of pain, and turn quickly to a new relationship instead. For many people, this very unsatisfactory process can transform into Change Addiction and continue *ad infinitum*, unless they take control of their lives and manage the change more consciously.

A similar scenario often recurs in business. Instead of the pain of first love, the individual may have real feelings associated with enjoying a meaningful job that came to an unsatisfactory ending due to changed management style, loss of promotion, bullying, or redundancy. Once again, to avoid the pain, as soon as the situation in the next job starts to resemble the previous scenario in any way, the individual will change jobs in order to avoid a repetition of the pain or humiliation.

If your lifestyle requires many changes, perhaps moving house frequently or taking a job that requires travel in many different countries, *plan your way* through this process to ensure that you do not become a Change Addict.

If you instigate a change *immediately*, revelling in the false belief that change itself is going to bring about the improvements you need in your life, you will probably be disappointed. The *action* of change does not bring about the positive improvement; your *attitude towards* the reason for the change is what makes the positive difference. In order to make positive progression and to reach a positive resolution, the positive Change Maker needs to strive for *Considered* Change in order to achieve a constructive result.

■ On the move

Carl was a warm and sociable person who had been born into an American Air Force family. His father's job meant that the family had moved home nine times by the time he graduated from college, and he had attended as many schools. He had lived in four countries and had first travelled on a plane on his own at the age of eight. In his early childhood years each new beginning had been difficult and each parting had been painful, but as he grew older he became used to settling in and enjoyed getting to know new people.

On leaving home he continued the peripatetic pattern without con-sciously realizing it, and by the time he reached his mid-thirties he had moved residence eighteen times, had held eleven jobs and had had a series of rela-tionships, none of which lasted longer than a couple of years. He was stuck in a place of zero-tolerance for emotional pain and his life had plateaued: no partner, no children, limited career progression, but a wealth of friends who continually lost track of where he lived and what he did.

When Carl learned the true power of Mind Maps at a Buzan Centre work-shop in California, he took to them with enthusiasm. He Mind Mapped his life and came to realize that in order to achieve what he really wanted – stability, fatherhood and a network of close friends – he needed to stay still for a time and stop 'running'. Positive by nature, he channelled the force of Meta-Positive Thinking to TEFCAS his way to achieving his goal. Five years on he has been working for the same employer for four years and has moved house only once more – after getting married. The couple have a firm community base and are now expecting their first child. Carl has transformed his Change Addiction into a channelled Vision and restricts his impulse for dramatic change to planning holidays and taking educational courses.

▓ Restoring the body positive

If we are born in physical balance, why and when do we lose that balance? At what point do we choose to stop running with the freedom of a young child? When do we stop interspersing our walks with skipping and jumping as part of the joy of traversing the distance from A to B? Why do we start to feel tired at the thought of raising ourselves from the chair in front of the TV to walk to the shops? What on earth possesses us to abandon the use of our finely tuned bodily machines and choose to travel short distances in a vastly inferior, man-made, motorized vehicle instead?

The process starts to go wrong when we feed the brain and body 'poison': when we reprogramme it with inappropriate information; when we modify the Radiant Thinking sunflower that is the human brain and force it into rigid, linear, monotonous, boring, restrictive, prison cells of thought. This alone debilitates the body system because when the brain becomes rigid, the body becomes rigid with it.

The body falls out of balance when we train it inappropriately in terms of physical health, or indeed don't train it at all. Modern-day school policy in the UK states that children need just *two hours* of physical activity *a week*; this highly restrictive guideline is applied at a time when the body is growing and developing the fastest.

The human body is designed fundamentally for movement. A body should regularly be given the opportunity to move, especially in ways that involve cardiovascular activity. We often develop negative habits in our own homes by spending hours immobile in front of the television or playing computer games, instead of enjoying aerobic activity and spending quality time outdoors.

If our bodies go wrong, our health and fitness will deteriorate and we will exacerbate the wrong formula. This is not malicious behaviour; this is not wilful destruction on our parts. We are simply trying to do the right thing in the wrong way, producing the wrong result and then believing the result is natural. In fact, what many of us have learned to do is change the perfect system with which we were born into an imperfect system. We then try to bolster or support our weaknesses, rather than making ourselves stronger and more balanced.

The universe has spent fifteen thousand million years designing us, and it has done a superb job; it is up to us to allow that continued evolution, to allow ourselves to change in a way that will enhance and optimize the performance of body and brain in tune with the way they were designed. We need to use our 'self' appropriately.

Being fit means that all your body's energy streams are flowing appropriately: the cardiovascular system, the immune system, the nervous system, the digestive system, your thoughts and your actions are all in harmony. If you are unfit it means that those systems are malfunctioning.

■ You are an Olympic athlete

Have you ever bemoaned the fact that you are feeling tired, run-down or lethargic? Do you wish you had more energy? The chances are that what you really need is better management of your change processes. If you are functioning optimally, the automatic result will be that you will have more energy.

If you were an Olympic athlete, would you train to become fit or unfit for the next Olympic Games? The answer is obvious. Of course, you would train to optimum fitness. To enter when you are unfit would be to risk grave physical damage and national and personal humiliation. *Not* a great result.

A Change Thinker will realize that *Life* is an Olympic-level competition. You are that Olympic Athlete. With that as your perspective, does it become easier to see that maintaining and enhancing fitness is your *only* option? Being unfit simply reduces the probability of your survival, reduces your chance of longevity, reduces your ability to bring about change, reduces your ability to keep taking positive steps forward – because you run out of steam, you become exhausted, and you get tired – you then get depressed, which means you get *more* tired.

The weary spiral is a negative, downward journey and of course you do change – negatively.If you have more energy you get more energy. The more motivated you are to change your life – the more you want to do something, the more energy you have – the better.

If you feel you have 'strayed from the path' of health and fitness, allow yourself to get back on track. If you are already fit and self-motivated allow yourself to believe you can be even better than you are, and try new ways of doing things, to become more creative in your successful endeavours. Remember: you are an Olympic Athlete, so Go for Gold.

Rebalancing health

Whatever area of your being suddenly becomes out of balance, whether it is physical health or psychological well being, it is important to redress the balance by strengthening all the other branches of your life and work to nurture back to health the branch that is weak.

The change challenge if you are suffering from illness is to keep your mind and body in good health. It makes good sense not to collapse into your weak 'Health' branch, just as you would not put all your weight onto a broken leg. Compensate for your temporary weakness by focusing on building your other strengths. Think back to the Victim and the Change Maker with the same type of hand injury in Chapter 7; you too can choose to gain benefit from your period of ill-health.

If, for example, you damage your leg, you may be tempted to think: This is disastrous; I will lose my short-term physical health completely. This is not true, as it is only your leg that is damaged. A former colleague who lost a leg as a result of late-onset diabetes took up kayaking. No-one meeting him for the first time would ever know he was not dual-limbed – an impressive example of personal triumph over adversity.

Many top athletes when they are injured find that the ongoing gentle exercises that they do to repair and maintain their overall body are as significant and good a training as those more vigorous exercises undertaken when they were in full health. The adjustment to their routine and the focus on the rest of the body actually strengthens parts that they had not previously strengthened. On returning from injury, their personal performance frequently improves to beyond former levels of fitness because they have developed and adjusted their routine. Those who collapse, put on weight, lose personal motivation and bemoan the cruel tides of outrageous fortune are changing in a negative direction and need to realize fast that they do have a choice.

The other essential component in achieving healthy balance is paying attention to your spiritual needs. This need not be in the context of organized religion, but involves becoming aware of your place in the context of your world, your society, and your universe.

■ The search for spiritual balance

Why is spirituality the next important element of Life Balance? Spirituality is your Big Picture. It's the Great Vision. Spiritual individuals by definition *always* have a Big Vision. The Change Thinker and Change Maker *always* have a Big Vision. They see their position in relationship to the universe. They also understand on a deep level that everything is related to everything else.

When you begin truly to *see* that vast breadth/ width/ distance/ depth of reality, you will experience a virtual 'yoyo' of perception as if you are operating as an alternating current, like a piston going forward and back within a machine. Look around you – when you see momentary changes, when you see cataclysmic changes, when you see problems happening, when you see seasonal changes, they are happening in the context of a constant. All this happens in the context of the Big Picture, just as the individual events in *your* life are happening in the context of the constant of *your* Big Vision.

If you have a Big Vision, you are stabilized in change. Spirituality gives you a base from which to navigate and negotiate the tides of flows and fluxes that are all around you. Spirituality will also involve an appreciation of, and usually a love for, other living beings. If you are walking around this planet, daily, with all the changes going on, and you reach out to everyone and every creature you see with love and appreciation and concern and compassion, you are going to bring about change in them because they will respond to that love, to that compassion.

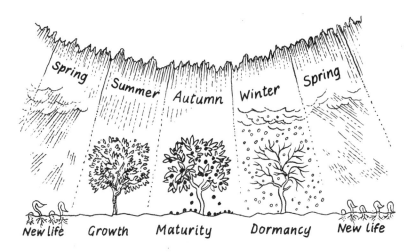

Each day of the year the plant cycle evolves from new life through dormant life in the context of spring, summer, autumn or winter, which are evolving under the constant of the Seasons. The constant of change is, as always, the non-changing element.Picture your life in this way. You are in a sense a gardener and you are able to nurture positive change. You will be able to handle and manage change yourself, you will be enthusiastic. You will have the energy, stemming from the energy of the universe, behind you and you will manifest that and influence others.

*If you can dream – and not make
dreams your master,
If you can think – and not make
thoughts your aim,
If you can meet with Triumph
and Disaster,
And treat those two impostors
just the same;*

...

*Yours is the earth and everything
that's in it ...*

Rudyard Kipling, *If*

Chapter 11
Change in business

❏ Work: a world of constant transformation

❏ Take stock of your working life

❏ Change and manage change

❏ Effective idea generation

You are now armed with the full range of Buzan's Tools for Transformation and nowhere is their success more quickly and more obviously measurable than in a business context. The world of business is an exciting example of constant transformation. The impact of business is felt in every corner of the world, from the very simplest bartering transaction through to the most complex investment.

The fact that everything is related to everything else is transparently clear in business. Witness the immediate impact on share prices if a company director is involved in a public scandal; think of the way house prices soar if there is talk of a boom in the economy; consider the ways in which the price of food commodities fluctuate in relation to the weather or natural disasters, and petrol prices soar in the light of international conflict; think of the impact that the positive attitude of a manager can have on raising the morale of an entire department – and how that has a positive and beneficial impact on the external reputation of the company.

Your role and success in business is a microcosm of yourself in life. You may consider life to be a business – the business of life. The different aspects of business that are acting upon you from your outer to inner circles of influence are:

Global business and forward trends
National changes in the political and economic arenas
Political influences at home and abroad
Environmental fluctuations both natural and man-made
Corporate business and levels of profit
Financial factors in investments and commercial trends
Leadership of the organization
Divisional management
Team behaviour
Relationships – yours
You – and your Vision of yourself

The point being that you have influence at every level of the organization you work within, and you can make a difference whatever the stage you are at in your career.

A Mind Map of the Aspects of business acting upon you

Buzan's Tools are highly applicable in a business context.

■ Your CTQ is a constant barometer of your Attitude to your work and how content you are in your role.

■ Without a Vision there is no business: no plan, no objectives, nothing for which to strive. Where you Focus your time and your ambition is crucial to your short- and long-term success.

■ The TEFCAS process is easily applicable and measurable in a business context. From the initial TRY to get your first job to the final SUCCESS of retirement, each and every day, each and every achievement follows an easily measured TEFCAS cycle.

■ Mind Mapping is the perfect tool to organize your personal work and to prioritize the use of your time, as well as being a highly creative and efficient tool for team working.

■ The effects of Meta-Positive Thinking – or its deadly opposite Meta-Negative Thinking – can make or break a company and, by implication, can make or break the individuals who make up that company.

■ Your Change Masters are immensely important in business. The role of mentors is now well established and can be particularly valuable for those at middle management level who are trying to influence the upper echelons while maintaining respect from the team. The personal characteristics of Change Masters are also critical in this area of life and it is worth reviewing them further in Chapter 8.

■ Getting into the Change Journal habit is a powerful way to manage and create Success in the career you aspire to and enables you to review the path you have travelled like a multi-dimensional CV.

■ Your self in business

Whatever the Change you are planning or facing, as you read this chapter, you will want to take stock of where you are and where you are headed in your career or work life. Focusing first on your current job or your desired profession as your Vision, select an image that is representative of your feelings about the Goal in the centre of your page. Decide on the branches for the Mind Map, based on considerations of:

■ What are the major elements in your professional life?

■ What is your actual job?

■ What are your goals within it?

■ What are your satisfactions within it?

■ What are your dissatisfactions within it?

■ Who are your friends and colleagues?

■ Who are your Change Master groups?

■ What is your environment like?

■ Is your income satisfactory and is it growing fast enough?

■ Are your colleagues people whom you enjoy working with?

■ Is the vision of your company congruent with your personal visions?

■ Are your bosses people whom you respect, look up to and who help you and nurture you?

■ What are your strengths and weaknesses, and what are the opportunities within your career path?

■ What are the threats to your chosen career path?

■ Are you seeking promotion – or no promotion?

■ Is the company liable to be taken over? Will there be redundancies?

■ If you are seeking a new job, what do you want from that new job?

Following the guidelines in Chapters 3 and 6, review the results and weight them. If necessary, Check them using the Change Matrix Wheel in exactly the same way as you checked the balance of your life. Undertake a Career health check, an MOT on yourself and your business. Decide to focus on those areas where you want to make improvements.

Make sure that the 'You' you are developing remains strong, healthy and focused by planning for time with friends, family or leisure pursuits. It is very important to integrate your life goals with your professional goals rather than allowing them to develop in conflict with each other.

Many people feel, without really thinking about it or monitoring it, that they *must* keep going up the ladder in business, even though this is often exactly the opposite of what they really want to do. They can become driven by the need for peer approval, status and money, even though they may prefer to use their business as a pleasant method of providing them with income while they have the energy to grow other aspects of their lives.

An individual who is true to him or herself, who is balanced, and who is managing change, will be better able to manage change in a direction that is in line with his or her preferred pathway within the organization.

It takes many people until the age of 50 or 60 to realize suddenly that they are spending the vast proportion of their lives doing what they do not want to do. Had they discovered the value of using a Mind Map and a Change Journal at an earlier stage in their lives, they would have identified this sooner and would have been able to bring about appropriate change.

Even at work you remain 'the captain of your ship, the master of your soul'. Once you realize this, you become a more valuable employee, because you will contribute with openness and with enthusiasm, because you are doing what you want to do, in conjunction with the goals of a company that you have chosen to work within, to bring about the positive changes in your life.

◼ International Trends in Business

The rate of change is not going to slow down anytime soon. If any-
thing, competition in most industries will probably speed up even
more in the next few decades.
John P. Kotter in *Leading Change* (1996)

John Kotter's statement sums up the reasons why we need to think more Flexibly, more Creatively and more Radiantly in business. Changes in business are happening at a speed never before experienced. We have been subjected to re-engineering, Just-In-Time techniques, Total Quality Management and a myriad of other methodologies for encouraging organizations to change in a commercially viable way.

Shona L. Brown and Kathleen M. Eisenhardt in their book *Competing on the Edge* (1998) identify two main theories of business change:

◾ Complexity theory – which in simple terms expresses the fact that order springs from chaos, the key to changing effectively is to stay poised 'on the edge of chaos'.

◾ Evolutionary theory – which is based on the Darwinian view that living organisms grow, adapt and change, evolving through natural selection ('the survival of the fittest').

The authors conclude that 'firms in rapidly changing industries are superior performers when they are able to combine these two processes and continuously reinvent themselves'. They are in a constant state of change but remaining stable within that change. Put another way: good business people have a hunger for lifelong learning.

What are the key changes in modern business? The changes include:

◾ Changes in the amount of information that is available.
◾ Changes in the technology.
◾ Changes in business practice.
◾ Changes in the language of business.
◾ Changes in the morality and ethics of business.
◾ Changes in the culture of business.

■ Changes in the financial structures of business.

■ Changes in the law relating to business.

■ Changes in the social environment of business.

■ Changes in political correctness in business.

■ Changes in different national approaches, and different racial approaches and religious approaches to business.

■ Changes in the role of the individual in business.

All companies are based on change. Just as Hyakawa San (see Chapter 1) could not put his foot into the same *river* once, so too are you unable to go to work at the same *company* once. All is change. Personnel change, thoughts change, external and internal influences change. You could sit at the same desk for twenty years and you would still experience radical change.

■ Have brain will travel

Every business was begun by a Change Thinker who transformed into a Change Maker. Every creation within every company was sparked by a creative visualization based on an 'aha' thought, in a moment, by someone or a team who thought 'we can change the way this business is done'. Even if they themselves did not understand the *process* of change, they had the great *idea* for change; they *started* the process of change. Most make errors. Some, but not all, have processes for checking their Feedback. Many companies do not check their Feedback, and they do not amass enough knowledge to Adjust their behaviour, which is why more than 95 per cent of companies started in the last ten years no longer survive.

Managing business change effectively is challenging. If change is too slow and too routine, there may be a downturn in creativity and individual resistance to change; a company that ceases to be flexible will lose its advantage in the marketplace.

If change occurs too fast – as a result of corporate merger, rapid expansion due to business success, or the need to downsize because of changes in the marketplace – a company will become highly vulnerable if it doesn't manage change well. The ramifications of this inevitably are that an increasing number of workers learn to adapt to ongoing cataclysmic change.

The brilliant employees take change on board as experience as they move on to the next job; they become people who develop multiple business intelligences, multiple skills. They are the burgeoning, nascent Da Vincis of the business world who can see the big picture; who know how to handle accounts, who know how to handle marketing, who know how to handle technology, who know how to handle people and sales. They become very, very flexible; they are like superb athletes who can excel in many different sports. Increasingly, these are the kind of people whom companies are desperate to employ.

Universities, colleges and cities around the world, but especially in America and Asia, are now seeking out and enticing a new generation of Change Thinkers to join them. There is a dawning of universal recognition that it is original thinkers who will create positive change for our future success. The signs are that if you learn how to optimize your creative ability and to manage yourself, your mind, your body, and understand your environment, you will be an extremely valuable resource and will be sought after and rewarded.

Whether or not it is clear to us all at the moment, with the advent of computer technology, and increased pressure on large business to reduce their 'overheads', there is an increasing trend towards becoming independent knowledge-workers rather than being individual cogs working within a giant machine. We are increasingly hiring out our intellectual or skills capital to the highest bidder and honing the unique selling product of our individual brains to the marketplace. If we manage this process, there is every reason why we can use this trend in congruent realization of individual personal life goals.

John Naisbett predicted that in the twenty-first century those who remain rigid, who are inflexible and will not change, will be the losers. 'Learning how to learn is what it's all about,' he said, at the launch of his book *MegaTrends 2000*.

■ Managing your business manager

If you are going to be a manager in a business context, then you have to further refine your management of your personal business manager, i.e. your amazing Brain. As we explored in Chapter 7, your brain is capable of a multiplicity of achievements.

Your brain has to manage you as Manager. It also has to manage itself as the Manager's manager. Of course, if you have a leadership role as well and you are influencing a large group, whether it be in business, in a university, an organization, a global movement or an army, your brain will have a whole matrix of other brains to manage.

The more of a leader you are, the more you will have to manage the management of your own brain, and the more responsibility you will have with regard to managing others, who have to manage *their* brains – their managers – and so on. There develops a wonderful cascade, a pyramid of brains all of whom are managing other brains. The ultimate manager of all those brains is the Leader. He or she is the manager of his or her own super agent for change – the brain. It is of vital importance therefore that the Lead Brain in any organization is a Change Thinker and a Mind Manager – no matter how large or small that organization is – because their input is directly affecting the thoughts, actions and reactions of many other people. The responsibility should be taken seriously.

▪ The individual and the team

Consideration of the relationship between 'the individual' and 'the team', in relation to bringing about change, leads us into the concepts of leadership and followership. As with all other aspects of change explored in this book, it is not the dyadic either/or because both are a requirement for change and stability. To be a good leader you need the capacity to be a good follower; to be a good follower you have to be a good leader.

To bring about change in a team situation, you have to be able to apply to the team all the things you apply to yourself as an individual to bring about change. You have to help that group of individuals in its Super-Individual state – the group, the team, the company – to achieve its goals. Exactly the same is true in a home situation where self-management and shared capacity for leadership are crucial.

Interestingly, field surveys I have done on this within companies show that individuals rate themselves quite highly in their ability as *personal* Change Makers to bring about change within their own lives. *However*, within the company context they rate themselves as relatively powerless; *they rate the company and its ability to change as low.* In other words, they think of their company as anti-Change Thinking and anti-Change Making and as rigid and conservative.

The fact is, of course, that *they are a part of the company*, and they should be applying their leadership ability and their skills to themselves and to the company in equal measure. The company, being a company of Change Thinkers, should be super-flexible and capable of dealing with change at extraordinary speed, in order to survive in the increasingly competitive and changing business environment.

The process of change in companies often appears more difficult than it is because there are company structures and processes to change as well. These changes can be s-l-o-w! If this is the case within your own department, why not use Mind Mapping to radiate a wealth of creative ideas for bureaucratic simplification and dynamic change?

■ Generating change across international boundaries

Alan Matcham of the Oracle Corporation was first introduced to Mind Maps ten years ago and realized immediately what an effective tool they are for capturing complex information in a succinct way. He values using them in his professional life because they awaken the imagination and engage the senses in a way that is much more effective than a linear technique. They encourage 'Aha' moments.

He became Director of Change Management at Oracle seven years ago and has used Mind Maps extensively as a method of planning and prioritizing, as a way of communicating complex ideas, and to combine different ideas from different parts of the organization. In the early days he drew Mind Maps by hand, but now makes increasing use of Mind Map software as the Mind Maps can then be communicated swiftly across the organization.

Sergio Giacolleto, Executive Vice President of Oracle Europe is also a great fan of Mind Maps, but Oracle has made no attempt to make Mind Maps a mandatory tool, believing that their benefits are self-evident and that their use must be a personal choice. Their obvious effectiveness has led to a rapid expansion of usage across the organization and a growing network of individuals now use Mind Maps to exchange ideas and present complex concepts.

Alan has used Mind Maps in particular for cross-departmental brainstorm-ing as they allow a particular problem to be 'thrown into the arena' and encourage individuals to add their solutions to the various branches over a period of time. Frequently this method leads to problem-resolution and the setting of clear priorities. Oracle executives are increasingly using Mind Maps in presentations because they can build a talk around just one slide; they are the perfect answer to 'death by PowerPoint'!

Alan Matcham has been liaising with ten of the world's leading business schools to introduce new technologies into executive education: IESE (Barcelona), INSEAD, London Business School, Nyenrode (Amsterdam), MIT (Boston), SDA Bocconi (Milan), EM (Lyon), JIM (Cambridge), Oxford Templeton, and Cranfield Business School. Mind Maps have been used extensively through this process and as an effective tool for change have enabled complex concepts to be transmitted with ease across territories, across language barriers, allow-ing issues of concern to be raised, communicated and resolved quickly. At a workshop in France two years ago, a group of sixteen professors, under the guidance of Alan Matcham, captured everything in Mind Map form: all sessions, all inputs, all outputs.

The use of Mind Mapping software is highly appropriate in an IT-literate environment where staff tend to be flexible, responsive and highly innovative. Alan Matcham values them particularly as a means of setting goals, and as a management tool that allows flexibility of response. According to Alan, they work as the brain works, making links in a non-sequential, non-linear fashion, connecting ideas and people to create greater value.

■ The role of the team in business

As a team member it is essential to realize that you as an individual can help make a team, or you as an individual can help destroy a team. The best member of a team is one who can lead when appropriate and who can follow when appropriate, and can help the team establish really positive goals.

If there is a dominant personality within the team, they are likely to infil-trate the team either with positive energy and enthusiasm that will enrich the team, or with negativity, pessimism and cynicism that will drain the energy of the team. It is important therefore, especially if you are aware of the power of your persona, to maintain a Meta-Positive attitude at work at all times.

Imagine a business in which every individual knew about Buzan's Tools for Transformation, knew everything we've been talking about here, and acted upon it. It would be a business in which every individual was a Change Thinker and Change Maker. Now imagine the opposite. For which business would you rather be working? Imagine the two businesses in a competitive business arena. Who would win?

Obviously the change-orientated company would be instantaneously and continually dominant. It is therefore of increasing importance for all companies to incorporate change and change management as part of their necessary core planning, focus and training.

Many businesses disintegrate because there are not enough positive Change Thinkers within them, but there are negative Change Thinkers all over the place, tearing each other's thoughts and visions apart. Big bankruptcies, big corruptions, are all based on lack of communication and a lack of ability to manage the process on an individual and team basis. Negative thinking can breed very rapidly, but only in an environment where such attitudes are not actively transformed into positive behaviour.

In an environment that knows how to manage change and what change management is, that knows about the processes of TEFCAS and Radiant Thinking and Mind Mapping and Life Balance, it would be very difficult to find a negative thinker amongst the Change Makers.

■ Effective leadership

To be an effective Leader you must have a clear Vision, and must have the skill and intelligence and charisma to be able to communicate that Vision to your team. It is essential in bringing about change, which is the lifeblood of any company, to make sure that all managers understand the value of leadership and its relationship to management and followership.

A Leadership Vision is, by definition, designed to bring about Change. In order for the Vision to be effective it is essential that you as Leader gather together as many others as possible who are enthusiastic and inspired *by* the Vision and who are willing to devote their (working) lives to helping that Vision become a manifest reality.

This requires a great deal of Trust. This trust has to be tempered with a very clear idea of what the Vision is and how to engage others in enthusiasm in a way that enables them to understand the *details* of the change, the *mechanics* of that change, and how they can use their own specific knowledge or genius to help manifest the Vision.

Crucial in bringing about the Change that will deliver a positive result is effective delegation. Delegation is the Achilles heel of many an otherwise inspirational and effective Leader/Manager.

■ The importance of being a travelling man

David Burt OBE was appointed Managing Director of Deutsch Ltd in 1990, and has subsequently become Chairman of the company. Deutsch designs and produces high-quality connectors for use in the aeronautics and automobile industries; it is renowned internationally for the quality and precision of the products and the professionalism of its service. David Burt says that this has not been achieved by standing still:

I am a travelling man. I use this phrase a lot. It means that I have not yet arrived. This is important when approaching the concept of change. It gives me the chance to evolve, and to progress change.

Change is something that the majority of people try to resist. I am a great believer in progressing the change processes by way of steps; I know from lengthy experience that expecting a straight line of improvement is unrealistic; it doesn't fit with behavioural patterns.

When you are facing change it is important to know what your core competences are. Too many people make change without understanding their core competence. As part of that process it is important to truly understand what the customer actually wants – not to assume you know what he wants. This gives the opportunity to evaluate the company's core competence against changing criteria. This is the most important key to survival in our business (and any business).

In 1989, 85 per cent of our business was serving the defence market. I saw no future in it. More importantly, neither did the public corporation that owned the majority of our shares. Today the defence industry accounts for about 15 per cent of our market. That in itself has, over 12 to 14 years, created a culture of change, some of it radical.

In 1989 we had no export business. Today the export market constitutes 31 per cent of our business. That is radical change.

In 1989 we had a turnover of £9 million and a range of established products, some designed more than thirty years before, which I was allowed to retain by our original public company in the formation of a new business. Today we have a turnover approaching £30 million, a high reputation for innovative new connector products, and an unchallenged reputation for quality. We listened to our customers and have changed our supply chain in line with changes in market requirements. Anything that gets the customer serviced in the simplest way with the least confusion is what we are each trying to achieve.

Prior to the demerging of the company I understood that the easiest way to manage is to downsize: cutting staff levels and reducing activity. This negative style of management, in an environment that is inevitably fraught with fear and concern about job securities, is hugely inefficient. Despite this difficult beginning the new company now employs some 300 people and we are proud of the fact that the average time served per person is over ten years. Although we have had some very harsh times we encourage a culture based on communication and belief in the achievement of success. Management at every level is kept as direct as possible. Each person takes responsibility within their sphere of influence and is accountable. Each member of staff is encouraged to see full parameters of the business.

A manager's role is to balance priorities and objectives, to evaluate risk in the long term and to use this information to motivate and encourage staff. Once the manager loses sight of these basic points he or she is in trouble. Short-termism driven by self-interest is no way to manage a developing business, and there are many examples in the public arena where managers have failed their companies with disastrous results.

Deutsch Ltd demerged from a £2 billion international corporation in 1989 and received the backing and support of the American Deutsch Corporation who took on the ownership of the company. They gave Deutsch Ltd a clear mandate to stand on our own two feet and did not attempt to get us to change the corporate objectives that we believed in. We have been able to build the business with the comfortable support of the Deutsch Corporation, which has helped to stabilize the processes of change tremendously.

People are the most important drivers of change. If you talk to your people you can make them believe in the vision of success. If they believe in success there's nothing that they will want more than to evolve the processes that will achieve change. One practical aspect of this is that the noticeboards on all Deutsch sites display a comprehensive, clean and detailed statement of all aspects of the company's activities. This information is provided routinely to all employees and is available to our customers, two days after the end of each trading month, so that everyone is advised of the status and performance of the company, whether good or bad. This format of reliable communication is an integral part of our success.

Managers who do not communicate are in trouble. It is a mistake to say 'I am the manager and I therefore want the following things done'. There is no better way of killing positive change and innovation.

Communication features consistently as part of our management and employment training. We liken communication to passing a heavy cannonball up and down a line of employees. If I am going to pass it to you, you have to know that you are about to receive it, be strong enough to carry it and know what you are going to do with it when you accept it. If you are going to pass it on you have to have someone else who is ready for the acceptance of it. If not – it will fall to the ground with a dull thud and probably land on your toe or mine. You have to provide structure. You have to have a whole network of people who understand what you are trying to do.

When you're dealing with corporate change you must have enough people with influence on board to embrace it; you can't do it as an individual. You must also be prepared to put in place an appropriate structure. Communication operates effectively through that structure. We spend a lot of money on training people how to communicate at all grades and every level. This means that we get natural feedback. Our staff have a direct say in their working environment.

The key to success is to make sure that the people with the right skills are in the right jobs, and to nurture self-confidence. Not everyone can be a goal scorer, some will be centre-forwards, and others will be defenders. Each member of the team needs to be in a role where they can perform to the best of their ability. The important thing is to let everyone know that goals are being scored and who has scored them. At Deutsch you see a lot of calm people feeling as if they are scoring goals. We have a good team; we all share in the same process, and we all share in the results.

Tony Buzan's *Tools for Transformation* are invaluable when used in conjunction with the evolutionary process of change within the company. TEFCAS and Meta-Positive Thinking are so much a way of life that I do not think of them as techniques; I use Mind Maps particularly when I am trying to 'paint a picture'. Mind Maps are highly effective in that they present complex ideas simply in a way that people understand and remember. The use of Mind Maps has percolated through the company because it is an appropriate working tool that people find they can use. The change is coming 'from the bottom up'. All change should manifest itself in that way: it occurs when people see the common sense of it, see the advantages of it and want to embrace it.

In our twenty-first century world, electronic communication cuts across country boundaries at a speed never experienced before. *The basic requirements of change have not adjusted, but in this explosive and fast-evolving climate it is vital to 'keep travelling', to constantly check and change your attitude to your market.*

Today, the process of making connectors is being challenged by changes in the supply chain. For example, Deutsch provides the majority of connectors for aerospace engines; civil or military in Europe. A connector is a crucial part of an aero engine, and our biggest customer is Rolls Royce (we have supplied them for 30 years). Rolls Royce are now beginning a process that will revolutionize the sales of engines. Aircraft are now sold without an engine. Engines will shortly be leased for the life of the aircraft via the engine manufacturer. The whole model for the industry is changing.

Deutsch are involved in this process on a strategic level through our business partners British Airways and Lufthansa because I am interested in how this process is likely to evolve. We have conceptually worked our way through the business model so that we can apply our support expertise to Rolls Royce. As the component manufacturer, this change radically affects our relationship with the supply base and will also affect the payment structure.

Fortunately Deutsch is very strong fiscally, and every employee knows it. It makes staff feel secure. This security will allow Deutsch the flexibility to remain stable during this process of change; and we will manage the process of change by being very selective. *If you focus on developing the wrong line, you wind up with a problem.*

Your relationship with your key customers is crucial. The more confident the customer is in you, the more successful you are likely to be in your change choices. We won't work with people who cannot work in partnership. That means developing a fully integrated procedure that allows Deutsch to develop our change programme whilst knowing what our partners are doing. A shared value system is important; it allows flexibility when things go wrong – and there will always be, in the process of change, things that go wrong!

The important thing in business as in all aspects of life is the relationship between the Mind and our ability to learn. Tony Buzan underlines my belief that the creative potential goes on and on. It has nothing to do with age. I am over normal retirement date and continue to work as efficiently and effectively as I can. I recognize that I have to match forty-five other Managers and Directors if I am to retain their respect; I am very fortunate to be 'driving the bus' in a professional sense. To keep me focused and in order to maintain life balance I take time to enjoy classic rally driving and I am also a very committed sculptor. I have a focused approach to time management and I enjoy retaining physical condition as a key part of being able to manage a long working day. As a general principle I do not start what I cannot finish.

I have now passed my management responsibilities to my battle-hardened and experienced team. We have worked together for many years, and the company's future is in safe hands. As chairman my job is to look to the future. I have become a mentor, just as each person becomes a mentor to another. We share experience, passion and loyalty for the company.

I cannot arrive. The day I think I have arrived somewhere, I am finished.

■ Creative thought in business

There is a common misconception in business management psychology, that the group brain is better than one, that more brains are better than one. This *can* be true with the right processes in place. However, it is *not* true when the many brains don't share a common Vision or where individual goals tear the centre of the group apart. Even a wonderful tool such as a Mind Map can become ineffective if the team who are using it in discussion get stuck in debate about minutiae over what colour a certain branch should be or which word should go where. Instead of an inspirational result, they will end up with something meaningless. In such a situation a single, directed, focused mind with a clear Vision would have been able to produce a better Mind Map than all of the others combined.

Uniqueness is a cornerstone of creative thinking.

In the contemporary business world, in the quest for the creation of multiple ideas, a group of twenty 'creatives' might venture off-site into the countryside to have an extensive 'brainstorming' session. Under the careful management of a Change Maker with leadership qualities, such a scenario has the potential to enhance radically the fortunes of any company.

The most conducive environment in the world will not help, however, if the leader of the brainstorming group stands at the front of the group and uses standard, linear, list-noting techniques to note 'all the best ideas' on a white board or a flip chart. This is because as each idea is written down in a linear fashion it will have the effect of cutting off the ideas already noted. The more each executive throws out ideas, and the more individual ideas are put up on the list, the more the group brain will be seduced into venturing down every one of the avenues suggested, enticed by those particular group thoughts.

Bright ideas

Try this as an experiment with your own staff. Divide your group into two teams. Encourage one group to think of ideas using the linear method and the other group to think of ideas using Mind Mapping. Give them five minutes. Which group generates the greater number of ideas in the allocated time?

It is normally considered excellent if a group of twenty individuals generates more than 200 ideas in a three-day brainstorming sojourn in the country. Estimate the cost-accounting expense of such a venture. If you send twenty brainstormers away for three days, you will incur the costs of their travel, accommodation and food, and there will be a cost for the individuals in being away from their jobs. In contrast, one individual, with the knowledge of how to manage change, with the tools to manage that change and the ability to Mind Map, can generate 300 ideas in half a day. Since Mind Maps are brain friendly and encourage Radiant Thinking, each one of those ideas will generate a multiplicity of future ideas. Thus the process accelerates over time, and one individual brain, using itself well, can outperform a group of twenty using an incorrect formula by a factor of 100.

Thus in any future organizational endeavour to bring about change, it is essential to teach each individual Change Manager (the human brain!) to process change management appropriately and then to combine that approach with other Change Managers using the same approach. If each one of you has the right methodology, each one of you will be able to contribute your universe of thought to the change process. You will be able to combine those universes profitably and as a team come together to forge the new Vision; and as a team you will come together to make sure that steps are in place to bring about that Vision.

In conclusion: more brains are not necessarily better than one.
More brains are better than one if each of those 'more brains'
is using itself appropriately.

Using Mind Maps as a tool for more effective brainstorming

Mind Maps operate in a way that is diametrically opposite to the gathering of lists. The Brainstorming Process for bringing about change with Mind Maps is based on the following steps:

Step 1. Individual brainstorm in the form of a Mind Map.
Step 2. Discussion in small groups of three to five people.
Step 3. Integration into single group Mind Map.
Step 4. Return to individual brainstorm.
Step 5. Incubation period.
Step 6. All small groups re-form into a single Group and create a conglomerate Mind Map.
Step 7. Final amalgamation of all thoughts by prioritizing and weighting the results for further action.

Mind Map software or simple self-adhesive notes can be used for this purpose. Decisions on how to act are then made on the basis of the considerations of all the individual ideas that have been generated. For each idea:

■ Consider
■ Refine
■ Select
■ Prioritize
■ Decide on a timescale

In this way, Mind Maps will bring about far more effective change.

In networking to discuss the ideas for your Vision, you are operating as a group like a Mind Map. You are a part and parcel of everything. Your actions and your radiant energy will affect those around you in a positive way. You will be creating a growing communal action towards positive change.

■ The stock market: a study in change

The stock market is a study of change. That's all it is. It's second-by-second change. The best leaders, analysts and traders in the field are also the best Change Managers. They are applying TEFCAS to their business dealings every second of every minute of every day. They look at all the data, they Check it, they get the Feedback, they Check it again, they immediately Adjust (Trade) in order to gain Success.

Business is change and that change both affects and determines the furthering of business. More importantly, the ways in which business views and talks about change, and the ways in which it is reported in the Press will often predict the outcome of business trends.

Business is *supposed* to be an objective scientific human activity, based on the laws of economics, but the laws of economics are fundamentally the laws of psychology. One only needs to read headlines in the major international broadsheets saying things like: 'Fear grips market' or 'Panic sets in' to know that, in reality, the attitude of individuals and groups of individuals to the events that happen in the marketplace is what really dictates the outcome.

The shout of 'US economy slows down dramatically', 'GNP improves by only 4 per cent' causes everyone to get depressed, and triggers the 'bears' and the 'bulls' of the stock market to stampede in one way or another. Much financial activity is the result of people panicking. Lacking in complete knowledge, and with no understanding of the process of change, they react in fear.

The great financiers, the great advisors – our modern-day philosophers, no less – have the wisdom to take the mid-term and the long-term view. They review the history of change, the patterns of markets; they look at the history of change in individual buying patterns and group buying patterns, and then, as well as they can, they *predict* when the next changes will take place.

Many financiers, understanding the historical information, will predict forthcoming change, and then manipulate the market, spread panic, and spread rumours that will result in that change coming about. They will have predicated their behaviour on what they predict the change is going to be.

The general herd will still be thrashing around, crying out: 'Property is going down' or 'My stocks are going down' or 'What am I going to do?' The general response is to 'Sell, sell, sell', and as a result, money is lost left, right, and centre. Meanwhile the long-term thinkers, who realize that change is a constant, will, like the surf rider, manage the rhythms well, and more often than not will manage them to their advantage, and not get caught. When they *do* get caught – predictions must sometimes inevitably go wrong – because they are Change Managers they can recover fast.

The encouraging fact now is that more than ever before in history an increasing number of individuals around the world are seeing and studying these patterns of behaviour.

■ High Fidelity

Bruce Johnson, who ran Fidelity, achieved an annual increase of over 10 per cent for twelve consecutive years in his funds. How did he do that? While everyone else was panicking, he would bring in to his office the top 30 advisors in the field. He would give them each two minutes to summarize what their thoughts were regarding the latest market knowledge and the action they would recommend. He used a giant Mind Map in the centre of his big board table to Mind Map everything they said. He would then send them all away and would apply *his own* knowledge and ability to the predictions. He would

integrate all their data, all their feedback and then he would make a decision.

It was the use of Mind Maps that allowed him to stabilize the rapidly changing tides of change and to predict where that giant river was going to flow to next.

To manage change in the business world you need to have as big and complete a picture as you can, with as much detail as is available, and enough knowledge about the direction and flows of human energy as possible, to increase the probability that the changes you predict will be so, and therefore your investment in those changes will produce profit.

■ The nature of corporate memory

Crucial to managing change in the business world is corporate memory. What do we mean by this? The word 'corporation' derives from *corpore*, meaning 'the body'. A business corporation is a body composed of the many individuals that comprise the whole, in much the same way as the human body is a corporation of trillions of minor or smaller bodies that work together to make the whole human being.

Just as the human body maintains its memory despite the fact that it is in a constant state of change – to the extent that all its molecules have changed over a seven-year period – so too a corporation is also in a state of constant change. Lack of awareness of the significance of Corporate Memory to a corporation has meant that, in times of continuing change, many corporations have offered their senior members lucrative financial enticements to encourage early 'retirement'. When large numbers or crucial members of staff leave a corporation the Corporate Memory is compromised. The corporation finds out within a very short period of time that it has lost entire databanks of crucial information from its Corporate Memory. The strategy is fatal.

The likelihood is that the members of the 'new' corporation will begin to repeat processes that are completely unnecessary. This kind of repetitive action would have been prevented had the original employee, with the memory of the results of the previous action, been able to give input. Ironically, many corporations that have 'retired' senior and technical staff are later forced, in order to reinvigorate their Corporate Memory, to hire them back as consultants at salary levels that are significantly higher than those they were receiving as members of the Corporation itself! The principle applies at middle management and administrative levels as well, where staff often act like the glial cells in the brain: i.e. the brain cells that hold the traditional neurons in place and allow them to function.

It is essential for business and governmental communities to realize that the Corporate Memory is a stabilizer in times of Change, just as the individual's human memory is a stabilizer in all situations of flux. Corporations need to develop methods of maintaining knowledge within the Corporation over time, while simultaneously developing systems that allow all members of the Corporation to access that entire body of knowledge. This is what 'Knowledge Management' truly needs to be about.

Knowledge management is the managing of the Corporate Memory and the application of that memory knowledge to address the problems of accelerating Change.

Are you aware of what you contribute to your corporate memory? If there is significant staff turnover, what steps are being taken to prevent the leaching of corporate knowledge and understanding at every level? What steps can be taken to ensure that your staff as individuals together develop the characteristics required of the new corporate brain?

The fitter and more agile you can keep your brain, and the corporate brain, the better your chances of being able to anticipate, adapt to and survive and prosper in change.

■ Intuition and change

An important part of that business 'big picture' comes as knowledge in the form of intuition. There is a mistaken concept that some people are logical and some people are intuitive and that never the twain shall meet. In fact, intuition can be considered a super-logic in which all our remarkable senses process trillions of bits of information and do a giant probability calculation that produces a somatic reaction. Business gurus such as George Soros and Peter Drucker have great respect for the power of intuition and recognize its contribution to their business success.

How does intuition work in reality? Imagine you walked into a social environment where you knew and liked many of the people. As you looked around the room assessing the danger levels and the pleasure levels, the probability calculation might be:

- Chance of survival in this environment as compared to all similar environments you have been in, in the past: 99.9 per cent.
- Chance of pleasure in this environment: 100 per cent.

You would then have a somatic reaction of elation and being receptive to the occasion, and you would be changing your response to the event as a direct result of your intuitive calculation.

Similarly if you walked into a hostile meeting and your senses took in all the information – the smell of the room, the movement of the people, the look of the people, the light, the physical structure and nature of the environment – your brain would instantaneously combine all those threads in a super holistic permutation. It would again 'print out' a probability. The probability printout this time might be:

- Chance of survival: 26.34 per cent
- Chance of pleasure: 0.1 per cent!

Your body would immediately react to this probability printout in the same way that your body reacts to *any* changing data that comes in. On receipt of this intuitive brain information you register 'pleasure' or 'pain' – attraction or aversion. You will get a 'gut feel', which is the body's somatic response to receiving changed data resulting from a paradigm shift of thought; whether that be an immediate paradigm shift, dictating 'Get out of here' or a mid-term paradigm shift, indicating 'Interesting to stay'.

Another way of describing this response is to identify it as a Super, Super-Logic. It is the brain's way of dealing instantaneously with change situations that put that body in a survival/ non-survival situation. It can also work to important effect in business, contributing to both corporate success and personal survival in the face of radical change.

■ Facing up to change

If you are a working professional, whatever your walk of life, you will be highly conscious of the infinite number of changes that affect you in your role on a day-to-day basis. It is perhaps in our working lives more than any other area of life that it can feel as if things happen to thwart our dreams and progress, that we are more acted upon than acting.

Mind Maps and your Mind Map Journal can be used extensively to rehearse your change options. For example, create a personal Mind Map if you're going to be promoted or if you want to be promoted.

Mind Map it if you want it, and then you make it happen.

If something has occurred that you would rather had not happened, Mind Map that as well, and then use the TEFCAS process to change towards a new goal.

Each time use the same procedure. There is one universal technology: TEFCAS combined with Mind Mapping. Use Mind Maps at each stage of TEFCAS to allow you to deal with whatever the situation is.

Referring back to your Mind Maps, identify the things that you CAN change and those you CANNOT. Bear in mind that *anything* is possible, in the right circumstances, so your CANNOTs could be transformed into CANs with some creative thought.

Referring to the change line below, which we first looked at on page 51, focus on the percentage that you can change and use it to influence the negative portion.

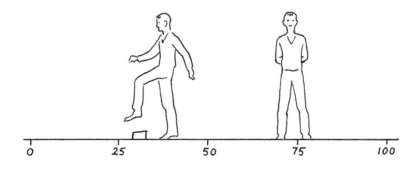

| 0 | 25 | 50 | 75 | 100 |

Place yourself in the mess of the negative side of the scale. Consider how bad the situation is and how it is making you feel. Note your:

- Posture
- Attitude
- Breathing
- Behaviour
- Communication

Of the factors influencing your mood, how many of them are positive?

Now use your brain to transform your mood and attitude. Imagine stepping from the negative to the positive part of the line. Note your:

- Posture
- Attitude
- Breathing
- Behaviour
- Communication

The likelihood is that you will be feeling more positive. Even though you have made no other changes, you have already begun to influence the connections in your brain.

Now you can see what a difference it makes to be in a position of Choice and to know that you have the option to choose your situation. You have the option of adopting a proactive persona, focusing on the percentage that is good in the situation, while still being quite realistic about the fact that a further percentage of your situation is pretty awful and needs changing.

■ Embracing redundancy

Perhaps the single greatest concern of employees in the twenty-first century is job security. As corporate mergers and takeovers become the norm, there is no longer any certainty of a job for life. Knowledge and worry about this can inhibit creativity and dynamic behaviour in some people; however, redundancy is a modern reality that *can* be embraced with positive heart. When talking about being made redundant, people invariably refer to 'the threat' of redundancy – and it can be a threat; for many it can also be a blessing – an excuse to rethink life goals and to plan to turn that dream into a reality.

Look back at page 65 and review the stages of loss and grief. These are very common amongst those who have been made redundant, especially if their life balance is out of kilter and their professional role has come to dominate their character.

■ Moving through change

Karin had worked in new business development for a sales company for many years. She was single and enjoyed a varied social life, but in the absence of children or a partner, she had committed heavily to making her way in her career. At the age of 45 she and one other member of the sales force were made redundant. It hit her hard. Her friends were deeply concerned at her withdrawal and negative attitude. In time, however, Karin began to emerge from her cocoon and with the help of her Change Makers and plenty of Mind Maps, realized that she had much to be grateful for and many benefits: enough money to reduce her mortgage substantially, or embark on re-training, more leisure time than she had had in her working life and the return of her health.

She enrolled on a training course to learn how to run her own business, took in a flatmate to help with cash flow and booked a holiday to the Red Sea to learn scuba diving. Six months later her former colleagues declared themselves envious that they had not been given the opportunity to do the same.

If you are managing change well, even when you are hit by a big wave of change, which can catch the unprepared person unawares, you will be able to regain your balance easily. You will be like the captain of a streamlined and powerful ship. Buoyancy will allow that ship to float and stabilize in the most violent of storms because it has the methodology, the energy to stay on top of it all, and because the captain has the brain and the skill to steer an effective course ahead of the waves. As an individual facing change you are not changing everything *suddenly*, you are changing while stabilizing: your body is stable through change, your need for nourishment is constant, your friends are both steady and developing, your learning capacity is constant while what you learn gradually evolves, your Mind Map stabilizer will remain in place, but some of the branches of your life will shift slightly in emphasis, depending on what *you* decide. Throughout life, you will remain a student, always learning, always accepting change, always embracing change.

■ Setting up your own business

Most employees with a number of years experience consider running their own business at some point in their working lives. Are you someone who has plenty of good ideas and would love to run your own business, but have concerns that you might not make it work financially?

A common hurdle to achieving change in a way that is personally constructive is fear of failure. The danger is based on the fear that you will 'set yourself up' for failure, especially if you feel you have experienced business 'failure' in some way before and are fearful that 'history will repeat itself'. How does this happen? It is related to rigidity of thought and lack of planning.

■ Having established a rigid, Utopian Vision of perfection, you may decide, either subconsciously or consciously, that the goal you have envisioned is unrealistic, that success is therefore not possible, and not bother even to try to embark on achieving it.

■ By embarking on your business change journey blindly, and with no clear plan of action, you may assume that you don't need to worry because everything along the way 'will be all right'.

In such situations many people become disappointed because reality does not match the 'dream of change'. There is an easy way around this: make sure your dream of change is a realistic one and that in planning for it you have, like any campaigner, prepared for multiple contingencies, both good and bad, along the way. If you are prepared for both successes and setbacks, then when either of these two comes along you will be prepared both intellectually and emotionally. Now that you are a Change Manager you can manage change of any sort. If your Vision is to set up and manage your own business, you will adopt the same rigorous process as for every other change in your life.

- Search for the arena in which you wish to make a change.
- Find the idea that you want to develop and make into an entrepreneurial adventure (add + venture).
- Create the best possible business plan and gain the best possible feedback from your Change Masters before investing a penny.
- Gather the appropriate team around you.
- Involve them in your venture fully by briefing them with a Mind Map of your short-, medium- and long-term goals.
- If you are going to be an employer, encourage each staff member to Mind Map his own goals and encourage a conscious TEFCAS procedure to make the changes time-bound.

If you continue to Mind Map your future for the business, pilot for success, successfully monitoring change as you go while incorporating all your new knowledge, there is every reason for you to become one of the beacons in your field.

Choose to think BIG
It takes less effort than thinking SMALL

Study Andrew Carnegie, study Watson, study Edison, study any major business innovator and you will find that what they did was obey all the principles of managing change, especially learning from their mistakes. If you look at their original Visions you will see that they were always *massive* change visions. Thomas Edison wanted to change the light of the planet at night; Henry Ford wanted to change the ability of members of families to travel to see each other across the vast expanses of the United States; Andrew Carnegie wanted to change the way in which the steel and oil industries were run and managed. The stories are wonderful and they are inspirational.

Andrew Carnegie

Andrew Carnegie, industrialist and custodian of wealth, is an excellent example of a Change Maker. He started life with nothing and as a young boy growing up in Scotland, he did not do tremendously well at school. From these lowly beginnings he determined to use his brain, literally, and his imagination to change his life – and this he did. He left Scotland for America, the land of opportunity at that time, and transformed himself very quickly by using his brain, his attitude, and the application of Meta-Positive Thinking to become by far the richest man in the world by amassing great wealth via the oil and steel industry. He is particularly interesting because when he reached the zenith of his commercial success, he looked around the world and realized that what was missing, globally, were educational and cultural institutions that could change the lives of those who would be otherwise socially and economically at a disadvantage. His philanthropic drive led him to invest extensively in libraries, museums, art galleries, cultural foundations, and any building devoted to the arts, culture, education and the sciences. He still ranks as the greatest contributor of the last 1000 years to world education and the bringing about of positive change through self-realization and self-enhancement.

■ The secret behind overnight success

The more I practise, the 'luckier' I get!
Gary Player

In the context of running your own business it is worth considering the concept of 'overnight success'. When a previously unheard of company explodes onto the international market with a new idea, and the marketplace recognizes the value of the concept, it is termed a Success. Many observers who were not previously aware of the company or the product will have the audacity to comment, 'How lucky' or 'So-and-so has become an overnight success!' Luck has *nothing* to do with it. Overnight success? It is important to understand that *there is no such thing*. 'Overnight' success is a delusion.

In every case that I have studied, 'overnight success' has resulted from the individual's perseverance: decades of blood, sweat and tears, and as a result of Try, Try, Try and Trying again, using the TEFCAS model, to Check, Check, Check on the Feedback, and Adjust, learn from mistakes, and re-focusing to keep the Vision going.

The good news is that each and every one of us has the capacity for persistence through TEFCAS – and so each and every one of us has the capacity to achieve true Success in business.

■ The business of life

We have a common tendency in our modern society to isolate business from life. We have tended to think of business as an abstract world over which we have little control, whereas we see our personal world as a much more warm, embracing world over which we have considerable control. The fact is, however, that business is a vibrant part of life, which in many ways can be seen as a microcosm of all other aspects of our daily lives.

In our daily lives we plan, create, remember, relate to other people, celebrate, become angry, get confused or lost, go about daily routines, change those routines, and feel frustrated or inspired.

In our business lives we do the same. To bring about more effective change in your business/ work, bear in mind constantly that you are much more in control that you may previously have thought.

Enjoy the team in which you work and help them change to all of your advantages: lead when you need to, follow when you need to; use Mind Maps to help you plan and stabilize your business and work life; relish your failures, learn from them and make them the basis of your next successes; create a Business Change Journal and use it as your friend, stabilizer and guide.

Always remember that you are the absolute manager of the ultimate business manager – your brain!

Once the realization is accepted that even between the closest human beings infinite distances continue, a wonderful living side by side can grow, if they succeed in loving the distance between them which makes it possible for each to see the other whole against the sky.

Rainer Maria Rilke

Chapter 12
The changing nature of relationships

❏ Your relationships with friends, family, colleagues and others

❏ Your relationship with your brain

❏ Choose to fall in love

❏ Combine energies for long-term effect

The word 'relationship' has come to imply 'love affair', but it is important to remember that we relate, we are in relationships, with everyone with whom we speak, everyone we work with, befriend, or are related to. We may adopt different roles according to the part we play in these relationships; however, the important reality at the core of each one, is our relationship with our true self.

■ Your relationship with yourself

On one level, you know yourself better than anybody else; on another more inspirational level, you are an untapped resource of utter brilliance, using less than 1 per cent of your current potential. If you have reason to be dissatisfied with yourself as you are at the moment, if you know that you are capable of more than you have achieved to this moment, then there is a wealth of opportunity to transform yourself into who you really are, who you really want to be.

If your relationship with yourself is in any way negative then you need to begin to improve it before you go any further. You have the choice to recognize and accept your essential self, choose to celebrate being alive and choose to realize your ambitions, maintain your body, your mind and your physical, mental and spiritual energies.

■ Understanding emotions

At the heart of all change are your thoughts, which lead to your emotional responses. While we are indeed the masters of our minds, we do not always feel in control of our emotions. Changes in our emotional responses can be the fastest, most subtle and most extreme of all. The whole of this book is therefore concerned with exploring and positively directing emotional thought pathways.

Your emotions are the driver, the motivator of feelings: the energy that draws you towards (and sometimes away from) change and your goals. Feelings are vital in that they inform all our actions.

Emotions are fuelled by Self-Talk. If you talk to yourself regularly in a negative way, you will chip away at your self-esteem, drain your positive energy, and over time increase and strengthen your negative energy. Negative energy is highly destructive; it shatters and destroys and relentlessly dismembers.

Think about the words that surround Negative Thinking. They are emotional words:

unhappy dejected sad pessimistic gloomy melancholic despondent miserable depressed

Can you feel your mood *sinking* as you read them?

If instead you talk to yourself in a Positive manner, you will develop Positive energy, its polar opposite, which will instead drive and propel, integrate, construct and create. The words that surround Positive Thinking are also emotional words:

cheerful pleased happy ebullient cheery joyful enthusiastic ecstatic contented

Can you feel your mood *lifting* as you think about them?

If your attitude is positive, encouraging and optimistic, your emotions and feelings will differ radically from those you will experience if your attitude is negative, cynical and pessimistic. Emotions are a product of your thinking. They are a function of your thinking and attitude to an event. The ability to feel is innate, but the feelings you have are a matter of choice.

Witness the classic example of two equally exhausted football teams at the end of an important football match. The winning side is jubilant, happy and energetic and can be seen running around the pitch in an energetic and victorious circuit. The losing side is bent double in the pain of exhaustion, or may be writhing on the ground; the body language is despondent, downcast and defeated.

The whole point is that both teams have been playing for exactly the same amount of time, in the same arena, for the same audience, in the same weather and one team has played harder than the other – obviously – because it has won. Yet the team that has spent more energy is even more energetic at the end of the game. The team that has spent less energy is less energetic. Why?

This is solely because of the mental attitude towards victory and defeat. A Change Thinker at the end of a game that has been 'lost' will react with exuberance, concentrating on the learning experience and looking forward to the Vision of being victorious in the next game and in the league. A Meta-Positive attitude in defeat breeds future success because the thinking becomes success-orientated.

Whether you choose to view something in a positive or negative way will depend upon your attitude, motivation and emotional concerns. The way in which you think, the attitude you choose to take, and the way you feel are intimately linked, just as the functions and effects of the circulation system and the endocrine system are linked.

In times of extreme change it may be tempting to be washed away in the tides, floods and the maelstrom of feelings. In bringing about change it is essential to understand that you are able to influence your emotions to make them Meta-Positive Emotions and to realize when you harness, create and nurture Meta-Positive Emotion, that you are providing yourself with the fuel, the energy and the dynamic force that will allow you to launch and propel your personal spaceship into perpetual orbit.

■ Your relationship with your brain

At the root of dysfunction, sadness and weakness in relationships is a brain that senses its ability and its potential, but which has been given 'evidence' that it is not good enough and that it is not worthy of success.

In the case of school children, the evidence is usually provided in schools as a result of tests which provide 'objective' confirmation that you are *not* intelligent, bright, creative or clever and are therefore seriously at risk in terms of survival. A highly able young brain will readily absorb and deeply understand this. The information feeds the primary relationship between the brain and the individual himself. On a secondary level this message also affects the relationship between the individual and society and his schooling.

On the basis of the external information the child has been given, he creates a self-image which becomes the 'real' person. The reason this may manifest itself as delinquent or depressed behaviour is because the brain fundamentally does not accept the negative image it has been given, and comes up with strategies to fight or defend against the negative image of the family situation. The fight against it is what causes disruption in society or in a relationship.

Trying to motivate someone in such instances can be counter-productive because if you begin to say to the child 'you CAN' and 'you're GOOD', when the child is constantly getting information to the contrary, the message will become distorted and the brain will understand that when people say 'you CAN', it actually means 'you CAN'T'. The only way you can really begin to bring about change in that person's relationship with you is by initially *accepting* their understanding of themselves.

I recently worked for a period of six months with a group of underperfoming junior-school children who had exactly this problem of negative self image. This work and its exciting and positive results became part of a BBC TV documentary called *In Search of Genius*. At the time I started to work with them, the children were under threat of 'exclusion' from school.

On my first day with them, I asked the children what particular problems they were experiencing with learning. They quoted back to me a list of negatives: 'I have a poor memory', 'I am doing badly at school', 'I can't concentrate'. They confirmed their negative image of themselves, and the fact that on one level they didn't think they could change.

I told them that I believed they *could* each improve and asked whether, if I gave them evidence, they would be interested in Trying to change. Unanimously they said they were willing.

If someone is lacking in confidence it is important to agree with them first of all, so that they know that someone is understanding what they are experiencing. You start off in agreement. Everyone understands the starting point.

The next stage is to look at some objective information about the way they work; the way they think; the way they function. In the case of the children, I gave tests. They performed badly on memory tests, they performed badly on creativity tests, and the results of those first tests confirmed their impression of themselves. They believed themselves to be underperforming and to have less than average ability. In response, I said: 'Let's have a look at the way that the brain works and see if it is true that your brain is not effective enough.'

The next step was to teach them how to do Mind Maps, how to use mnemonic techniques to improve the function of memory, to teach them how their brains work, to give them Change Masters: heroes and heroines. We then agreed to apply the Tools for Transformation appropriately in order to work in a way that was commensurate with the brain's function, and in order to Try to change the situation that each child believed him or herself unable to change, i.e. academic performance, social performance, creativity and memory.

Once I was confident that they had mastered the techniques, we revisited the tests they had done before. Each child could see for him or herself that there had been an improvement; their image of themselves was being contradicted by their improved performance. The results placed doubt in their minds and the doubt was a *positive transformational doubt*. They suddenly began to doubt that they were who they thought they were and what they had been told they were. They began to see that the dream they had of improving themselves was possibly an achievable reality.

When you laugh with children, show them that you care and are committed to them, and give them tools for change, they will bring about changes in themselves. They will bring about changes that are immediate; changes that will transform in the way that 'everything connects to everything else'. Each child's behaviour changed, their health changed, their immune systems changed. Over time, their friendships will also change, their understanding will change, their outlook on life will change. Already, each child's personal Vision has transformed and become bigger.

The child's relationship with its teacher in this process is similar in principle to the relationship between a child and a mother or a friend and a friend. One has to:

- Commit to the individual.
- Agree with them on the desire for change.
- Help them see the possibility of change.
- Begin to change their self-image first of all.
- Help them by providing them with tools for transformation – of all sorts.
- Commit to them over time, to be their friend, guide, coach, companion, through the ongoing transformation of their lives.

Your relationship with others

Relationships are essential to life. We are connected to each other in ways that are both mutually dependent and independent. In the same way that all of life is in constant flux and change, so too relationships between people are constantly changing. Elsewhere in *Embracing Change* we have explored the fact that we as organic beings are constantly striving for homeostasis, for stability in the midst of change, that change is a constant; nowhere is this more apparent than in our quest for relationship with others.

The art of changing relationships relies largely on our ability to hone our social intelligence. The more adaptable we are to changes in our surroundings and the more open we are to new experiences, the more we will be comfortable in the company of others, whatever the situation. We can learn to use our entire body and brain to communicate with others.

Here are a few pointers:

First Impressions The majority of our communication is through body language – and as we all know, first impressions count. So smile!

Active Listening Making use of your ears and your brain will allow you to communicate in an empathetic and totally engaged way. You have one mouth, but two ears! If we each use our ears twice as often as we use our mouths, our understanding and learning abilities would increase a millionfold. Your brain can think at least four times faster than your mouth can speak, so the more you listen, the more time you have to think, and the more involved you can choose to become.

Individuality Your ability to shine in a unique way, congruent with your own personality, is your key to personal, professional and social success.

Self-confidence Your ability to think in a Meta-Positive way will have a direct bearing on your attitude to yourself and to others.

Kindness You can change the nature of your relationship with others in powerful and simple ways through the gift of kindness. The moment you put another person's needs ahead of your own, you change everything. Whether you offer a small gift of appreciation or take the trouble to put someone at ease in a social situation, your feelings about yourself, their feelings about you, and their feelings about how they will react to others alter immediately.

Leadership Recognizing the extent of your personal influence. By this I mean the act of taking responsibility for your actions, for the needs of others, for the way you think and react to everyone around you.

The more we recognize that we are *personally* responsible for the vast majority of things that happen in our lives, the better able we are to respect our fellow human beings, to extend the hand of mutually respectful relationship and to lead *ourselves* appropriately.

No-one else sees the world as you do. You have a perspective that is unique to you and valuable to others. The same is true for everyone else too – and it is useful to remember that!

■ Business relationships

'It's not what you know, it's who you know', as the saying goes. In the competitive environment of the twenty-first-century business world, you can be sure that 'what you know' is of vital importance too, but what the adage expresses effectively is that those who have influence make the decisions, and by implication those who make the decisions like to work with those they feel an affinity with.

To achieve the positive change you want in your business life, therefore, it is important to be aware of the value of a few basic social principles:

■ Be aware of the vital importance and impact of first impressions and last impressions. Your boss and your colleagues will remember the way you were the first time they met you AND the last time they saw you.

So, use your individuality and professionalism to make sure those memories are positive.

■ Be positive. Develop an attitude that is optimistic and constructive.

■ Keep your body language open, not closed – especially in meetings.

■ ACT with confidence – regardless of your emotional state.

■ Focus on the other person first. Become genuinely interested in other people.

■ Smile! It will mean you become known as someone who is approachable. This means you will be kept better informed about what is going on and will be thought of in a positive way.

■ 'Get a life!' – outside your work. You will be a more interesting colleague if you have something other than the latest business project to talk about.

Honest and genuine adoption of these principles will lead to effective business relationships in your workplace, and make you memorable when networking in the broader business arena. Improving and enhancing your interpersonal skills will enable you to change to become whoever and whatever you want to be.

■ The value of friendship

If a man does not make new acquaintances as he advances through life, he will soon find himself alone. A man should keep his friendships in constant repair.
Samuel Johnson

As you evolve through life, you will experience many things and may have the opportunity to visit many places. With every new door that opens you will make more acquaintances: some will be children, some will be your peer group, some will come from an older generation, some will become important lasting friends, others will be transitory. Whatever their context, whatever their generation, the social skills that you would apply in a business context are even more important where your friends are concerned. These are the people who will provide you with your anchor in times of trouble, your true Feedback when Events have not turned out as you had hoped, and who will encourage you to keep Trying in your quest towards achieving your life goals.

Your friends are quite simply the Change Thinkers and Change Makers who have the greatest influence on your thoughts, your attitudes, your levels of self-esteem and your likelihood of achieving successes in life. Your influence on their lives is similarly powerful.

■ Family relationships

These principles apply to relationships within families too. Families take many different shapes and forms, but whatever form *yours* takes, your family relationships will be a constant in your life from birth until death.

Both nature and nurture have a vital role to play in influencing our upbringing and determining who we are. How we respond to this and how it influences our lives will be different for each person in the family unit, and will change over time.

■ Same family: different perspective

Parents are frequently bemused by their children. They say such things as, 'I can't believe Teresa [aged fifteen] and Mike [aged twelve] are growing up to be so radically different; they are experiencing the same upbringing, they are treated exactly the same, they go to the same school …'

It is impossible to have the same view of the world as another human being, no matter how closely related you are. Each family member has a different set of relationships; each family member experiences a different family. Teresa is the only female in the family who is living with a younger male sibling. She is the only one in the family who has never seen her face across the meal table, she is the only one in the family who is the eldest child and is the only one who sits where she does in her classroom each day, has her set of friends, and experiences her relationships with the teachers. Likewise, Mike is the only young male in the household influenced by two older female relatives. He is the only one who has not seen his face and his facial expressions, other than in a mirror. He is the only sibling without a younger brother. They are in the 'same' family, but their worlds are radically different; therefore each needs to be respected for their differences and treated as a unique and precious individual.

Each individual is unique: an 'entire universe capable of a number of thoughts equivalent to the number of atoms in the known universe' (*New Scientist*), and the Change Thinkers we call our friends and family are more unique than any stone is or any mineral is. What do we call these unique minerals? 'Gems', 'jewels', 'precious', 'rare', 'beautiful', 'valuable', 'priceless'. It is therefore appropriate, when dealing with other people, to remember not only that they are unique in their ability to think and that they are infinite in their ability to change, but also that with their individual behaviours and their internal universes they are rare and precious creatures.

Relating to children

Children are our future – our genetic future, our societal future, and our commercial future. They are also our heritage: the fruits of our labours, the result of our influence, the next generation of growth when our generation is in the winter of its life. You don't have to be a parent yourself to have a responsibility towards the children of our global future. We are their guardians and their Change Masters. It is vital that we give them every opportunity to experience life changes in a positive and nurturing way.

Many parents make the mistake of trying to control children in ways that prevent them changing. What the 'good' parent needs to do is to allow the process of change within the child to develop and flourish like a flower. Children are creatures of vast, fast and constant change. They are like us, and we have been like them, but they are also experiencing life in a completely new and unique way that we can never experience.

As a parent, watching your young child grow and change, you will experience supreme joy and may also have times of poignant sadness as you long for your child to stay as they are: small, sweet, charming, unique – and dependent. Do not be tempted to strangle those moments of joy by looking backwards, or suffocate your joy by looking too far forwards. Enjoy the enjoyment, enjoy *them* enjoying, enjoy *their* enjoyment, and let them be free to enjoy in their way, not necessarily in your way. If you 'kiss the Joy as it flies' there will be ever more joyful times to follow.

He who binds to himself a Joy,
Does the winged life destroy;
He who kisses the Joy as it flies,
Lives in Eternity's sunrise.
William Blake

William Blake is being super-subtle here. He is saying that joy *will* come to you. As it flies by you, kiss it, thank it, embrace it, and release it. Let it go, because there will be more and more and more moments of joy, *if* you are looking towards the Vision, *if* you are looking towards the future, looking towards Eternity.

To help children develop the qualities and strengths you strive for yourself, encourage them to use Mind Maps from a very early age to develop the ability to focus and harness the untapped genius and wisdom of the childhood imagination and to manage change.

The Tools for Transformation are both simple enough and powerful enough in their simplicity to be used with ease by any age group. Children are so fast and so adaptable in their approach to learning that they will understand how to use them almost immediately.

■ Choosing to fall in love

No chapter on change and relationships would be complete without a section on romance. Emotion is a matter of attitude; it is also a product of both bio-physiology and biochemistry. It is born of a reaction to your intuition and a reaction to physical changes in your body. The simple fact is that you can *choose* whether or not to fall in love. People get very emotional about this, and the reason why they get emotional is that they are checking their databases, coming up with their probabilities, thoughts and opinions, and reacting on the basis of those. Falling in love is an emotional response to your thought processes. It is intuition – your super-intelligence – in romantic action.

Falling in love through the feeling of physical attraction is a mental process; it is also a biochemical, hormonal response. It's a wholly sensual response to a multitude of stimuli; it is also a predilection or a mental preference, linked to a series of associations that have influenced your thoughts and responses throughout your life. For example, if you become aware of the first sexual response of your life and the person who has triggered that response has long hair and is wearing blue, you will always associate blue and long hair with that first sexual impact. So it is not 'innate'. It is trained, and is trained by you.

The minute you realize that, you can start to be much more in control of your feelings, you can actually let your love express itself much more completely.

Loving relationships are another example of constancy and change. The individual whom you love will be changing second by second; you will be striving to keep your love as a constant within this constant of change. Shakespeare expresses this beautifully.

Let me not to the marriage of true minds
Admit impediments. Love is not love
Which alters when it alteration finds
Or bends with the remover to remove:
O no! it is an ever-fixed mark
That looks on tempests and is never shaken...
William Shakespeare

▓ Changing your 'luck' in love

Understanding the important role the mind plays in your emotions is crucial if you have ever thought of yourself as 'unlucky in love'. The good news is: there is no such thing! If you have experienced the feeling of being in love then that can never be termed being 'unlucky': You met someone who you felt was wonderful, you enjoyed ecstatic times and then with regret you may have drifted apart. How lucky to have had that joyous experience.

If falling in love is your goal, then make sure you Focus on your Vision and ensure that everything you do conspires to help you to achieve your goal. Mind Map your aspirations. They could be to improve your levels of fitness, to overcome shyness, to socialize more widely, to learn to dance or play sport, to enhance your social skills. Whatever it is you need to do to bring about positive change in yourself, which will influence your attitude and therefore your attractiveness, needs to be on that plan for action. If you are not sure why you are not achieving success, then ask those Change Masters who would be best able to help: your siblings, someone whom you were involved with previously, a close friend whom you can trust to be forthright and honest with you, a professional counsellor. No more 'I'm not *this*', 'I'm hopeless at *that*', 'I'm too *x*, *y* or *z* to find love.' Listen to the Feedback with all your senses and commit to adopt Meta-Positive Thinking to keep you firmly on the TEFCAS Change Trail.

■ The ending of a relationship

Feelings transform and change, and the love between two people is not always enough on which to build a lasting future. When a relationship ends it may be a time of great sadness, particularly if there is the pain of divorce to contend with. However, when two individuals decide to go their separate ways, it can also be a very *good* thing – even if it doesn't feel that way in the early stages of change. It is a New Beginning for both people.

Even though both people in the relationship have been unhappy, or thinking about change, it is often the case that one person in the relationship becomes the Change Maker and takes the definitive action to bring it to an end. It is a mistake for the non-change thinker to believe at this point that, because their partner is changing, he or she does not love them, did not love them, has never loved them. This is not the Truth.

The Truth is that for one, two, ten or twenty years, each of you decided that the other person was the one with whom you most wanted to have your closest relationship. You enjoyed all kinds of fun, all kinds of excitement and closeness, all kinds of paradise moments. You will also have had painful moments, some unpleasant moments and some 'warning' moments of Adjustment, telling you that all is not well. All of that is permanent. It will always remain a major part of your life. So, rather than enter the negative spiral of destruction and blame, why not have as your Goal the wish to keep that person as a much-loved friend so that you can reminisce – if not immediately, if not soon, then in the future?

In other words, review the wonderful things that you did together, laugh at the tragedy and the comedy of some of the things that you did. Check your memory of the Events. Get Feedback from each other. Ask him, ask her:

'What was the cause of you shouting so much?' 'Why did you decide to go off with person x, y, z?' Not in order to stir up old arguments, not in order to accuse, but to gain Feedback, via pure TEFCAS.

If the person is truly your friend, and they probably are your friend, they will understand why you need to know, and they will tell you. If they are not truly your friend, if they become antagonistic and dismissive in the face of your question, then you have a really good piece of Feedback: 'How was I able to choose this person as a companion for this period of time, when in reality I didn't know who they were?' In other words, what was this blind spot in me? What did I see in them, what was really wonderful about them and valuable about them? How can I learn from this experience to enrich and improve my future?

■ A marriage of minds

Aimer, ce n'est pas se regarder l'un l'autre;
c'est regarder ensemble dans la même direction.
(Love does not consist of gazing at each other;
but in looking together in the same direction.)
Antoine de Saint-Exupéry

If you are within a relationship, you must take account of the needs of the other person as well as your own. This may mean taking *more* account of his or her needs than your own. The relationship in which you are involved is going to change both from your partner's point of view and from *your* point of view. It is the Goal of both people in the relationship to find the constants that you want to have in your relationship, to decide what things there are that you and they feel are the most important.

Many people, particularly in young adulthood, swing wildly from one relationship to another because they are not actually thinking about what they really want, either as individuals or as a couple. They are going for the quick 'love affair', they are attracted by the physical or material attributes of an individual, they are not exploring the relationship, they are not exploring the changing dynamics of what happens between two people, they are not exploring their own strengths.

If you and your current partner share your lives, then your separate paths of change are intertwined and shared in a way that is both forceful and challenging. Think back to the metaphor of the two rivers in Chapter 1. There will be periods of great excitement and turbulence as well as the possibility of long-term peaceful and powerful flow as you combine your energies to long-term effect.

Mutual Mind Maps

To help you combine your energies in a synchronized and Radiant Thinking way, explore your joint ideas and ambitions for mutual change through Mind Maps.

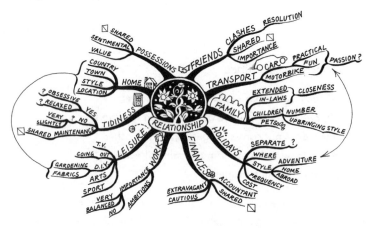

Agree on your headings. Then create two separate Mind Maps (no conferring!). Take stock of the results together by creating a third Mind Map that summarizes both your areas of agreement and convergence and your areas of difference and divergence.

The areas of difference are as valuable as the areas of convergence and are important areas of individuality that will feed and challenge the growth and development of your relationship. Use TEFCAS to agree a way forward. Make sure that you are both applying Meta-Positive Thinking to both your relationship and your aspirations.

Create a Journal to map your progress and to create a joint record of the journey you have shared, which you can review for both practical and sentimental reasons as time goes on.

▓ The value of memory in relationships

Memories are your constants in life: the memory of your great romance, the memory of watching a special sunset, the memory of your closeness and your times together. If you keep your memories as a constant, they will always provide you with honest feedback, whether positive or negative.

It is your relationship with your memories that changes over time, not the memories themselves.

Memories only change over time if you encourage them to do so, if you don't treasure them and preserve them in their pristine form. There is a tendency, if you are not thinking consciously about your relationship and as you become involved in one spiral or another, to change your perspective on what happened, to believe what you *want* to believe. This will serve you badly. A false memory gives you a false perspective, which is unhelpful to you and your future well-being. Photographs, videos and love letters can help to keep memories intact. Maintain the purity of the positive times and use the painful aspects of the relationship to inform and guide you in your ongoing relationships, and in your ability to help other people who get stuck in the same turmoil.

There are those who feel 'held back' by memories, who avoid preserving their memories because they are afraid of being drawn back to the past and the pain they felt then. This occurs only if you are *mismanaging* your memory and you don't know how to get the positive Feedback from those memories.

Mind Maps are a wonderful way of preserving memories, and your Change Journal is an ideal method of recording the processes of your change and recording your improvements.

- ▪ Gather the moments of joy and happiness.
- ▪ Keep the memories accurate.
- ▪ Learn from the lessons of the past.
- ▪ Apply all your knowledge to a better future.

If you *understand* your memory, then reviewing your past to preserve the pristine nature of the Truth of your life in the form of Mind Maps, photographs, letters and records will be to maintain a valuable archive, a physical memory, a tool for auditing the past and moving towards the future.

Life can only be understood backwards, but it must be lived forwards.

Soren Kierkegaard

Chapter 13
Embracing ageing

❑ Milestones of transformation: your personal evolution

❑ The route to renewed innocence

❑ Learn and relearn

❑ Ageing is all in the mind

During the course of our lives we each experience significant changes that mark milestones of transformation. These are times when we are particularly in tune with the change that is happening; when we are observing ourselves consciously as 'different' from how we were previously. As a result we relate differently to those around us and their response to us also changes.

The 'natural' course of change steers a powerful and steady course through life. It is an irony that from the moment we are born we get closer to the moment when we will die and transform into another state as yet unknown to us.

■ From Zorba the Greek by Nikos Kazantzakis

I remembered one morning when I discovered a cocoon in a bark of a tree, just as a butterfly was making a hole in its case and preparing to come out. I waited awhile, but it was too long appearing and I was impatient. I bent over it and breathed on it to warm it. I warmed it as quickly as I could and the miracle began to happen before my eyes, faster than life.

The case opened, the butterfly started slowly crawling out and I shall never forget my horror when I saw how its wings were folded back and crumpled; the wretched butterfly tried with its whole trembling body to unfold them. Bending over it I tried to help it with my breath. In vain.

It needed to be hatched out patiently and the unfolding of its wings should be a gradual process in the sun. Now it was too late. My breath had forced the butterfly to appear, all crumpled, before its time. It struggled desperately and, a few seconds later, died in the palm of my hand.

The little body is, I do believe, the greatest weight I have on my conscience, for I realize today that it is a mortal sin to violate the great laws of nature. We should not hurry, we should not be impatient, but we should confidently obey the eternal rhythm.

During gestation, over a period of nine months, you evolved steadily and remarkably in the womb. At the time of your birth you moved literally from one universe to another, and on entering the environment we know as our world you instinctively learnt how to express your needs, and quickly learnt to eat, crawl, walk, talk, run, skip, and to laugh. You were designed to endeavour and to improve and to feel ecstatic at your discoveries.

During your personal evolution through childhood to adulthood you experienced a number of further transitions from one form to another. Even now you are in a perpetual state of metamorphosis, as if in transition from pupa to chrysalis, chrysalis to butterfly. If you are alert to them you will experience exquisite and beautiful, if transitory, 'butterfly transformations' constantly, each of which provides opportunities to learn and re-learn.

As we transform, we also seek bridges or role models in order to link our worlds. If we are fortunate, we will find bridges that have been engineered by those who preceded us – by our Change Masters and mentors. On other occasions we may need to build our own. These bridges represent periods of transition and take different forms at different times in our lives. One may take the form of a physical transition such as adolescence or menopause, another might be an event in the form of a chance encounter or a milestone birthday, a crisis in the form of an accident or an unplanned change of job, or anything else that represents a period of taking stock, consolidating, plateauing, before moving forwards again. Throughout the experiences of age and ageing we will transform using TEFCAS.

As we grow we will progress through states of Innocence through Experience and then return to Innocence again, so moving towards the same goal but at a higher level.

Innocence and experience

If the doors to perception could be cleansed
we would see the universe as it really is.
William Blake

A Change Thinker who uses creative thought to bring about change is constantly striving to see the universe as it really is, and in this way is able to 'cleanse' the doors to perception, to show the universe to those around them with new perspective.

William Blake, the great English artist, poet and visionary, introduced a wonderfully clear, powerfully subtle concept that reveals our capacity for constant learning, relearning and effective change. He developed as a major theme in his world famous works *Songs of Innocence* and *Songs of Experience* the states of Innocence, Experience and (renewed) Innocence.

His poems emphasize that in the first state, **Innocence**, the baby or child is totally open, totally curious, totally explorative and beautifully naïve. As life progresses, bringing about changes and the accumulation of knowledge, behaviour changes from the more open to the more 'learned'. We gain **Experience**.

Over time, these changes are sifted and winnowed by the ever-changing brain, the less viable of them being discarded, the more viable being maintained and enhanced by memory. Thus in each phase and stage of our lives we pass from Innocence to Experience.

Once the initial experience is assimilated, we become ready to move on to the next stage. We are entering fresh, unknown territory. Experience transforms into **Renewed Innocence**.

The whole of life and all our individual lives are moving in an ever-renewing transitional cycle, which is in itself made up of many smaller cycles, demonstrating this concept.

In the wonderful quote on the previous page, William Blake is saying that the way in which we see things is unclear and that to gain clarity we need to change ('cleanse') the ways in which we observe and experience life (our 'perception'). This relates again to the transformation of Innocence through Experience. Innocence transmogrifies over time into Experience: Experience being the clouding of the Vision. To cleanse our perception and to gain clarification we need to refocus on the Vision, to regain a form of Innocence; to change our perception back to what it was, in the context of an advanced state of consciousness.

When was the last time you did something for the first time?

The Path of Change through life as followed by the good Change Thinker will lead the interested traveller to a series of 'new dawns' in which all senses will once again open wide, curiosity will re-establish itself, and the mind, the body and the spirit will transform to a new Childhood, a new Innocence that is supplemented and enriched by the best and most appropriate knowledge of change and how to manage it and appreciate it.

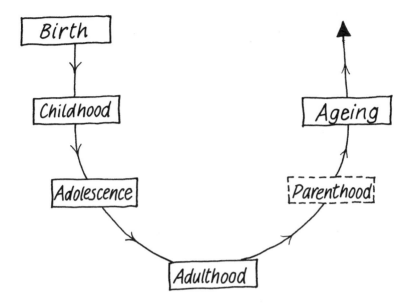

■ Tony's memory of history

My relationship with history began at school in **Innocence**. I was an enthusiast – interested in everything, and ready to learn whatever was taught to me – until I was presented with the sheer grey monotonous drudgery of the way history was taught and presented to me at that time.

Boringly presented events and disconnected dates seemed to bear no relationship to me, my life or indeed my future. It seemed impossible to connect with anything meaningful in the subject. My **Experience** of history led me to jettison it with delight from my academic curriculum as soon as I had the opportunity. This state of Experience continued for some years.

It was only in my mid-20s when I had begun to develop my interest in and passion for the subject of memory, that I had an epiphany – a revelation. *History was the memory of the human race!* If history was memory, and the topic of my most fervent interest was memory, then I must also be interested in and love the study of history! I reached a new state of open-mindedness – a state of **Renewed Innocence**.

The path to Renewed Innocence through Innocence and Experience can be used consciously as a highly original and creative Change Management technique. Every time you are confronted with a situation of change that needs to be managed by you, approach it with the eyes of a child – in innocence and without prejudgement. Supplement the problems and challenges inherent in the situation with appropriate knowledge, but as you move into the next stage of 'non-knowing' approach it with candour and clarity – with renewed innocence. You will increase the chances of managing the change to your and your future's advantage.

> **Maintain Innocence in understanding and a freshness of approach in all things, in order to proceed from Innocence to Experience and onward to Renewed Innocence.**

If you can learn to see your world with Renewed Innocence, you will constantly change and refresh your Vision in order to strive for and realize your own personal 'paradise' – your goals, your vision, your dreams.

Learning and Relearning are the prime methodologies for dealing with growth and change throughout the course of your life, whether in the workplace or at home. To deal with change, you need to be able to hold your position steady on one level (keeping your eye on your Vision), while also being flexible (via TEFCAS) – much as a willow tree deals with dramatic change.

■ The willow

The willow tree is a wonderful metaphor for the ability to remain still while moving, and while growing, especially in the most dramatic times of change, just as we stay the same and yet are flexible and grow through life. It is also a metaphor for strength, based on its ability to move and flow as opposed to being rigidly strong. In the wildest storms many tall, stout and inflexible trees are destroyed. The willow, apparently weaker and more frail than other trees, is able to become wildly flexible while simultaneously remaining firmly rooted.

It exquisitely combines stability and movement: the trunk and branches are more flexible than those of other trees, giving it structure, form, safety and *security*. Change Thinkers and Change Masters are like willows – flexible in approach, while grounded in TEFCAS and the structured approach to change.

■ The third age: the age of Renewed Innocence

Ageing is traditionally perceived as a time of physical deterioration, of retiring, of slowing down, of 'looking backwards' and, if we are lucky, of enjoying our grandchildren. There are many, many misconceptions about getting older. There are many people who do not follow the conventional 'retirement' route. They may carry on working, begin a course of study, undertake a new venture, set up their own businesses, travel around the world, learn new languages and new skills. Perhaps they have always wanted to garden and so they become gardeners; they might write a book, or they may decide suddenly to learn to paint.

Ageing is an exciting process of personal transformation and challenge which can be embraced and enjoyed with as much vigour and hopefully fewer traumas than in the teenage years.

The key is to embrace the present moment, and to recognize that, in order to achieve a sense of equilibrium and balance you will need to change – in a way that *you* choose.

As in the previous sections, the tools of Mind Mapping, TEFCAS, Meta-Positive Thinking, Planning, and Keeping a Mind Map Journal can have an immensely beneficial effect on the quality of your later years.

Mind Map Your Senior Years

Whatever your age now, pause to draw a Mind Map of what *you would like* your 'old age' to be like. Bear in mind that while in good health, we rarely believe that we have arrived at the point of old age, no matter what age we are. I hope I can safely assume that your imagination still perceives it as some time off.

In the centre of the Mind Map, start by drawing an image that encapsulates your idea of old age. Then from here branch out to develop your Vision.

Now – check your Mind Map.

For the central image, have you used one of the classic images of the elderly? Bent double with a stick, in a wheelchair, in a rocking chair, with a Zimmer frame, in a graveyard, or as a skull and crossbones? You haven't? Congratulations – Meta-Positive Thinking is at work. If you have – and many people do – consider for a moment the gap between your conditioned image of getting old, compared with your personal aspirations. Begin from this moment to Focus on your positive aspirations for your personal 'third age' and you will banish the cliché permanently.

On the branches, have you outlined positive and active goals such as: travelling, enjoying grandchildren, gardening, rediscovering music, new romances, financial security, using knowledge to help others, learning at least two major new things each year?

It is important to re-emphasize here that your big Vision is always directing your energy and activity. If your Vision of yourself in your later years is one that directs you towards becoming crippled and bent, then that is where you are para-consciously guiding yourself. For most of the last two centuries this has been the normal global image of age, and because of this, most people have transformed into a real-life manifestation of those various images. It has been assumed that it is natural for a human to change and evolve in this way. In fact, it is not natural and it is not what you need to become. Ageing is all in the mind. Those who embrace change positively are people who will be forever young, whatever the state of their physical body.

Use Mind Maps and TEFCAS to ensure that your actions take you in a positive and constantly healthy direction. Use Meta-Positive Thinking to keep negative images at bay and use your Change Journal to chart your ongoing transformation to new states of Innocence.

■ New friends, new experiences

A possibly unexpected change during retirement is that you will (hopefully) have a sudden vista of free time. For many people, used to the frantic routine of their busy lives, this can be overwhelming in its potential for choice, when in fact it is a gift of paradise that takes you back to childhood and offers scope for the making of new friends.

You may think: I've got my lifelong friends, I'm now too old to make new ones – but in fact, the freedom you have is akin to that in your first day in kindergarten. You are meeting a whole range of new children with whom you are entering a new phase, and are going to play, fight, explore, laugh and cry. If you consider your retirement in this way, you will gain the nervous anticipation and energizing sensation of starting again, and of finding new friends and new vistas.

Remember, as I outlined in Chapter 7, your attitude depends totally on you. There are those who allowed their work to become their life, who find when they retire they have nothing left to live for. Why? Because they were totally unprepared for change; they unwittingly slipped into the swamps, the tar pits, like the dinosaurs, without even realizing they were slipping into them. Suddenly to have no authority, no daily routine, no computer, no company car, no personal expenses, no personal phone – is a shock, and they are transformed. They don't know what to do, or how to handle the change.

What's your Attitude? Are you prepared for it? Your Mind Maps will act as the icon for your Vision, a constant beacon towards which all your mental and physical energies sail.

If you're a Change Manager or a Change Thinker in transition from your paid working life to the next stage in your life, remember you are simply transferring to another department in the university of life. You're still a full-time student, you're just shifting the emphasis of the way in which you study and learn.

You have the opportunity to change your activities, to rediscover dormant abilities, to allow your wishes and dreams to come true, in the sense of taking up those things you've always wanted to do. You can choose to transform yourself – in any way you want.

Embracing your future

You've come to the end of *Embracing Change* and are about to continue the ever-changing journey that is your future life. Having read *Embracing Change*, you will meet your future with an enhanced ability to mould, sculpt and direct your life as a Change Agent and a Change Master. You are now equipped for your travels and journey with an enhanced ultimate Change Agent: your brain. You have an increasingly fit and flexible mind and body, an improving self-esteem, and, as travelling companions, your Tools for Change.

Your Change Thinking Quotient will provide you with a constantly improving base from which you will be able to accelerate your positive change. Your increasingly refined and clear Vision will act as a beacon, constantly drawing and accelerating you towards your goal, while simultaneously helping you to overcome obstacles. TEFCAS is your physics-based gift from the Universe, allowing you to multiply the trillion-fold information received through your senses, and to direct it towards your vision.

The Mind Map is your ultimate thinking tool, and your prime tool for recording your Change Journal, a Master-Level Diary that will help you record, clarify and magnify the effectiveness of your tools for transformation and your success in life. Meta-positive Thinking will bring into alignment your brain cells – the world's ultimate workforce – all now working for you.

Supplementing all this and acting as virtual Warriors of the Mind on your behalf are your Change Masters: towering icons of Change Mastery who will continue to strengthen your enthusiasm, your commitment, your creativity and your persistence and stamina. They will also help you to take risks in pursuit of success. They will further provide you with a constant and optimistic view of life, while providing you with many moments of joy, fun and laughter.

And living increasingly in the moment you will be increasingly spanning eternity. You are the captain of that spaceship that is your mind and your body, driven by your now increased energy and enthusiasm.

The Universe awaits you!

Recommended Reading

Use Your Head, Tony Buzan, BBC (London) rev edn 2003
The Mind Map Book, Tony Buzan, BBC (London) rev edn 2003
Mind Maps at Work, Tony Buzan, HarperCollins (London) 2004
Use Your Memory, Tony Buzan, BBC (London) rev edn 2003
Master Your Memory, Tony Buzan, BBC (London) rev edn 2003
Speed Reading, Tony Buzan, BBC (London) rev edn 2003

Business titles

Leading Change, John P. Kotter, Harvard Business School Press (Boston, Mass.) 1996
The Heart of Change: Real-life stories of how people change their organizations, John P. Kotter, Harvard Business School Press (Boston, Mass.) 2002
Competing on the Edge: Strategy as structured chaos, Shona L. Brown and Kathleen M. Eisenhardt, Harvard Business School Press (Boston, Mass.) 1998
On Becoming A Leader, Warren Bennis, Random House, Arrow (London) 1989
The Age of Unreason, Charles Handy, Random House, Arrow (London) 1989
The New Leaders: Transforming the Art of Leadership into the Science of Results, Daniel Goleman, Time Warner (London), 2002
How To Win Friends and Influence People, Norman Vincent Peale, Random House, Vermilion (London), 1993

General

Passages: Predictable crises of adult life, Gail Sheehy, Bantam Books, 1977
New Passages: Mapping your life across time, Gail Sheehy, 1997

Literature

You may enjoy reading about change through these great writers
William Blake
Ovid: *Metamorphoses*
Rudyard Kipling: '*If*'
William Shakespeare: his Sonnets and Plays
Sun Tse: *The Art of War*
Antoine de Exupery: *The Little Prince*
Lewis Carroll: *Alice In Wonderland* and *Alice Through The Looking Glass*
John Bunyan:*The Pilgrim's Progress*
Vladimir Nabokov: *Speak, Memory*
Marcel Proust: *Remembrance of Things Past*
Works by J.J. Sarre: *Snap*, *Dragon*, *Solstice* and other novels

Further Resources

Dealing with Problems & Change: Your 'First Aid' action booklet, Vanda North, The Buzan Centres (Poole) 2004.
Get Ahead: Mind Map Your Way to Success, Vanda North with Tony Buzan, The Buzan Centres (Poole), 2001
Map it! MindMap Software, BrainPower Ltd, www.mapitsoftware.com

Index

Buzan centres

For information on all Buzan products and courses

Email: buzan@buzancentres.com

Website: www.buzancentres.com

UK

Buzan Centres Ltd Headquarters
54 Parkstone Road, Poole
Dorset BH15 2PG
Tel: 44 (0) 1202 674676
Fax: 44 (0) 1202 674776
Email:buzan@buzancentres.com

USA

Buzan Centre USA Inc
PO Box 4
Palm Beach, Florida 33480
Free Toll in USA (1) 866 896 1024
USA (1) 734 207 5287
Email: buzan@buzancentres.com

Make the most of your mind today